# Praise for *The Tourette Syndrome and OCD Checklist*

"This book is truly a work of art, heart, and science!"
    —Barbara J. Coffey, MD, MS, director, Tics and Tourette's Clinical and Research Program, New York University, Langone School of Medicine; associate professor, Department of Child and Adolescent Psychiatry; research psychiatrist, Nathan Kline Institute for Psychiatric Research, New York University Child Study Center

"This is a fantastic book full of wit and wisdom from an educational pro. I have known Susan Conners for over twenty years and have had the good fortune to watch her speak and engage an audience. If you don't get a chance to see Conners in action, this book is the next best thing. Her depth of knowledge and capacity to make a difference in the lives of children shines through on every page."
    —John T. Walkup, MD, professor of psychiatry, and director, Division of Child and Adolescent Psychiatry, Weill Cornell Medical College; chair, TSA Medical Advisory Board

# Jossey-Bass Teacher

Jossey-Bass Teacher provides educators and parents with practical knowledge and tools to create a positive and lifelong impact on student learning. We offer classroom-tested and research-based teaching resources for a variety of grade levels and subject areas. Whether you are a parent, teacher, or another professional working with children in grades K–12, we want to help you make every learning experience successful.

From ready-to-use learning activities to the latest teaching framework, our value-packed books provide insightful, practical, and comprehensive materials on the topics that matter most. We hope to become your trusted source for the best ideas from the most experienced and respected experts in the field.

# The Tourette Syndrome & OCD Checklist

## A Practical Reference for Parents and Teachers

Susan Conners

Foreword by Dr. Cathy Budman

JOSSEY-BASS
A Wiley Imprint
www.josseybass.com

Published by Jossey-Bass
A Wiley Imprint
989 Market Street, San Francisco, CA 94103-1741—www.josseybass.com

Jossey-Bass books and products are available through most bookstores. To contact Jossey-Bass
directly call our Customer Care Department within the U.S. at 800-956-7739, outside the U.S. at
317-572-3986, or fax 317-572-4002.

Jossey-Bass also publishes its books in a variety of electronic formats. Some content that appears in
print may not be available in electronic books.

Library of Congress Cataloging-in-Publication Data
Conners, Susan, 1948-
  The Tourette syndrome & OCD checklist : a practical reference for parents and teachers/Susan
Conners; foreword by Cathy Budman.—1st ed.
    p. cm.—(Jossey-Bass teacher)
  Includes index.
  ISBN 978-0-470-62333-6 (pbk.)
  ISBN 978-1-118-07527-2 (ebk.)
  ISBN 978-1-118-07528-9 (ebk.)
  ISBN 978-1-118-07529-6 (ebk.)
  1.   Tourette syndrome in children.   2.   Obsessive-compulsive disorder in children.
  I. Title.   II. Title: Tourette syndrome and OCD checklist.
  RJ496.T68C66 2011
  618.92'83–dc22
                                                                    2011011122

Printed in the United States of America
FIRST EDITION
PB Printing      10  9  8  7  6  5  4  3  2  1

# About This Book

Tourette Syndrome (TS), obsessive-compulsive disorder (OCD), and the other associated neurological disorders discussed in this book are some of the most baffling and complex disorders currently known. They are also some of the most misunderstood disorders you will encounter. Children with these disorders can be challenging to both teach and parent because of the complexities and the ever-changing nature and severity of their symptoms. Unless you have walked in the shoes of these children, it is very difficult to truly understand how disruptive these disorders can be to the individual who has them. It is equally difficult to know how to accommodate these symptoms without enabling the child. It is my hope that this book will:

- Teach you what Tourette Syndrome and OCD are and, just as important, what they are not
- Help you understand the impact of these disorders on all aspects of a child's life
- Dispel the stereotypic myths about TS and OCD
- Give you practical techniques, strategies, and accommodations for both educating and parenting children with these disorders
- Assist you in obtaining school services and creating an appropriate education plan and placement for the child
- Help you see the child and her strengths, not just the symptoms of her disorder

# About the Author

**Susan Conners, MEd,** is a nationally and internationally sought-after speaker, teacher trainer, and author on the topic of the education of children with Tourette Syndrome (TS), obsessive-compulsive disorder (OCD), and other related neurological disorders. She has presented hundreds of conferences and workshops in forty-eight of the fifty states, in Canada, Puerto Rico, Spain, and Norway. She was a multiaward-winning middle school teacher for thirty-three years and has TS, OCD, and learning disabilities herself. Her work focuses on educating educators about the complexities of TS and OCD, providing common sense and effective accommodations and strategies to help students with these disorders to be successful, assisting educators in developing positive behavior intervention plans, and helping to change the way we look at children with this spectrum of disorders.

Conners has authored many articles and brochures and produced videos on this topic. She has appeared on and served as a consultant for several national television programs on TS, including ABC's *20/20, The Geraldo Show, The Montel Williams Show,* ABC's *The Practice,* the BBC Discovery Channel, the Emmy Award–winning HBO documentary on Tourette Syndrome (*I Have Tourette's, but Tourette's Doesn't Have Me*), and ABC Primetime's Emmy Award–winning documentary (*Living with Tourette's*). She served on the national board of directors of TSA, Inc. for twelve years. She was the founder of TSA of Greater NY State and has served as its president for twenty-five years. For seven years following her retirement from full time teaching, she was employed by national TSA, Inc. as their Education Specialist. Susan continues to work as the volunteer president of TSA, Inc. of Greater NY State and as a private consultant and speaker across the country.

# Contents

**About This Book**                                                v

**About the Author**                                              vi

**Foreword**                                                     xiii

**Preface**                                                      xvii

**Introduction**                                                   1

**Section One: Basic Information About TS,**                        3
**OCD, and Associated Disorders**

1.1.   What Is Tourette Syndrome (TS)?                              5

1.2.   Manifestations of Motor Tics                                7

1.3.   Manifestations of Vocal Tics                                9

1.4.   Waxing and Waning of Symptoms                              12

1.5.   Suppression of Symptoms                                    14

1.6.   Other Related Tic Disorders                                16

1.7.   Medical Treatment of TS                                    18

1.8.   Associated Disorders                                       21

1.9.   What Is Attention Deficit Hyperactivity Disorder           22
       (ADHD)?

1.10.  Dysgraphia                                                 24

1.11.  Executive Dysfunction                                      27

1.12.  Depression                                                    29

1.13.  Sleep Disorders                                               30

1.14.  Sensory Processing                                            31

1.15.  Learning Disabilities                                         33

1.16.  Auditory Processing Difficulties                              34

1.17.  Social Skills Deficits                                        35

1.18.  Behavioral Issues                                             36

1.19.  What Is Obsessive-Compulsive Disorder (OCD)?                  39

1.20.  Manifestations of OCD                                         40

1.21.  Medical Treatments for OCD                                    46

1.22.  Behavioral Interventions for OCD                             47

## Section Two: Understanding the Impact of TS and OCD                  48

2.1.   Why It Can Be Difficult to Recognize TS and OCD              49

2.2.   The Impact of TS and OCD on the Family                       50

2.3.   The Impact of TS on School Performance                       53

2.4.   The Impact of OCD on School Performance                      55

2.5.   Tips for Accentuating the Positive                           59

2.6.   Tips for Ensuring Success at School                          60

## Section Three: Checklists for Parents                                62

3.1.   What Parents Can Do at Home and at School                    63
       to Support Children with TS and OCD

3.2.   Preventing Meltdowns Through Positive Behavioral             65
       Management and Supports

3.3.   Accommodations, Tips, and Environmental Changes   69

3.4.   Managing Homework   73

3.5.   Suggestions for School Breaks, Rainy Weekends,   76
       and Summer Vacation

3.6.   School Issues   79

3.7.   Synopsis of an Individualized Education Plan (IEP)   80

3.8.   Tips for Being an Effective Advocate   82

3.9.   Sample Letter for Requesting an IEP   84

**Section Four: Checklists for Teachers**   85

4.1.   Top Ten Things Teachers Need to Know About   86
       Tourette Syndrome

4.2.   Tips for Working with Students with TS and   88
       OCD in the Classroom

4.3.   Tips for Training Staff on Working with Students   90
       with TS and OCD

4.4.   Tips for Educating Peers About TS and OCD   91

4.5.   A Peer In-Service Model   93

4.6.   Strategies for Dealing with Motor and Vocal   98
       Tics in the Classroom

4.7.   Accommodating Motor Tics   99

4.8.   Dealing with Vocal Tics   101

4.9.   Accommodating Vocal Tics   102

4.10.  Attitude Is Everything   103

4.11.  Classroom Observation Form   104

4.12.  Tips for Addressing Challenging Behaviors   105

4.13. Functional Behavioral Assessment and Positive    106
Behavior Intervention Plan for Students with
TS, OCD, and ADHD

4.14. Accommodations for Associated Disorders    116

**Section Five: Other Helpful Checklists for Parents**    126
**and Teachers**

5.1. Educational Rights of Students with TS and OCD    127

5.2. Individuals with Disabilities Education Act (IDEA)    128

5.3. What Is a 504 Accommodation Plan?    132

5.4. Requesting Services    134

5.5. Sample Physician's Letter    135

5.6. How to Proceed If You Disagree with the School's    137
Evaluation

5.7. Being a Role Model for Children with TS or    139
OCD and Their Peers

5.8. Relaxation Techniques    140

5.9. School Placement    141

5.10. Sources of Help and Support    142

5.11. Recommended Organizations, Web Sites, Books,    143
Videos, Articles, and Brochures

**Appendix: Real-Life Scenarios**    **147**

Motor and Vocal Tics    148
   Tap, Tap, Tap    148
   "I Have a Chicken in My Pants"    148
   PB and J    149
   The Dreaded Cursing    150

Head, Shoulders, Knees, and Toes 151
Where Should Jeannie Sit? 151
No Applause Necessary 151
Self-Abusive Tics 152

## OCD and Anxiety 153
The Clipboard Chronicle 153
Dairy Dilemma 154
Locker Phobia 154
Toeing the Line 154
Why Theresa Feels Trapped 155
Can You Hear Me Now? 155
What If I Choke? 156
"But You Promised Chicken" 156
Kids Don't Tell 157
To the Point 158
Thank God for Purell 158
Scantron Saga 158

## Dysgraphia 159
When Writing Hurts 159
Photo Op 160
To See or Not to See 160

## Behavior Plans 161
Hash Browns, French Fries, or Tater Tots: Any Kind 161
of Potato Will Do
The X Box Does It 162

## Miscellaneous 163
I Like Ben Better 163

## Executive Dysfunction 164
A Shoe Will Do 164
Circling the Wagons 164

## Index 167

I would like to dedicate this book to my two Marys: my best friend for twenty-five years, Mary Lohrman, and my younger sister, Mary Conners. I lost both of these two beloved people in the past three years and both at much too young an age. My friend, Mary, was one of the most extraordinary women I have ever met—a teacher, a mom, and a humanitarian. We spoke every day, sometimes for hours. Her passing left a huge hole in my life that can never be filled. Everyone should be as blessed as I was to have such a wonderful friend.

My sister, Mary, was my hero. Most people in this world faced with the many obstacles that she had to overcome in life—TS, OCD, depression, and a significant hearing loss—would have sat back and let the world support them. Instead she chose to go back to school, earn her bachelor's and master's degrees in her late forties, and go to work as a mental health counselor helping others. It was the unconditional love and friendship of these two ladies that was "the wind beneath my wings" as I wrote this book.

I would also like to thank my beloved Andy who has shared my life for sixteen years through good times and bad. He will hopefully be at my side for many more years to inspire me to continue the work that I do.

# Foreword

For many educators, parents, and health care professionals, symptoms of the neurological disorders Tourette Syndrome (TS) and obsessive-compulsive disorder (OCD) are difficult to recognize and understand. Rigorous public health efforts have increased awareness of the now well-established neurobiological and hereditary under-pinnings of TS and OCD. Yet without the benefits of truly meaning-ful support and interventions, many people with these conditions continue suffering from dramatic and more subtle disruptions of daily life.

As a specialist who has diagnosed and treated many children and adults with TS and OCD for over twenty years, I know this to be true. The first person with Tourette Syndrome I encountered during medical training in the mid-1980s was a twenty-six-year-old man with TS. He was misdiagnosed with schizophrenia as a teenager because of his sometimes bizarre repetitive involuntary utterances and move-ments. Frustrated by his problems concentrating and rejected by classmates, he eventually dropped out of school, only to languish for over a decade in a state mental institution before his neurological symptoms were finally diagnosed and treated.

At that time TS was still believed to be quite rare; milder cases were largely unrecognized, particularly in school settings. This point was particularly emphasized by the highly gifted and uniquely qualified educator Susan Conners when she presented at a major conference on TS and associated disorders at our institution in 1994. A teacher, a school administrator, and, most important, a person who had lived with TS her entire life, Susan translated and taught us about the internal and external worlds of TS. Her charismatic personality, humor, and keen insights were riveting. At one point during her talk, Susan invited the audience (composed of health care professionals, educators, and families) to temporarily experience life as a child with TS in the classroom. She asked us to perform a seemingly simple task: to write down the Pledge of Allegiance. However, Susan also instructed us to blink our eyes and erase the words we were writing every time we heard her clap her hands, which she proceeded to do at irregular and unpredictable intervals. Needless to say, few, if any, of us were able to complete the task in the allotted time. We learned firsthand how a relatively effortless exercise or action can be transformed by tic and/or obsessive-compulsive symptoms into a frustrating, arduous challenge.

It was also Susan Conners, in her capacity as the National Tourette Syndrome Association's education committee chair, who offered testimony to Congress in 2001 that helped lay the groundwork for TS to be correctly recognized as a neurobiological condition, leading to its inclusion for the very first time in 2004 in the definition of Other Health Impaired (OHI) for the Individuals with Disabilities Education Act (IDEA). This landmark decision made it possible for children with these impairing neurological symptoms to receive the necessary modifications and supports to learn effectively and thrive in the classroom.

Now, in this beautifully comprehensive and practical guide, Susan has drawn upon her considerable professional and personal experiences with TS to deliver a detailed road map for parents and educators. This text provides relevant background on Tourette Syndrome and its associated disorders, informs and promotes understanding of what these symptoms are and how they impact on the individual at home and in school and, most important, provides specific tips and recommendations for effective support and interventions.

As you read and refer to this book, realize that Susan Conners is an expert guide who has issued us a temporary visa to visit, tour, and experience the world of TS. Unlike Susan and many other people with TS, however, the reader can enter and exit this world at his or her own free will. Take time to absorb the multitude of information and advice that is expertly organized here into useful sections for easy reference and teach your children well.

I am grateful to Susan Conners for enlightening families, schools, and health professionals about what it is like to have this disorder, what makes things worse, and what makes things better.

Cathy Budman, MD

Director, Movement Disorders Center in Psychiatry

Associate Professor of Psychiatry, Hofstra University School of Medicine

Manhasset, New York

# Preface

At age six I was already beginning to exhibit symptoms of Tourette Syndrome (TS): eye blinking, head jerking, sniffing, and squeaking sounds. Despite many, many visits to a variety of doctors over many years, it was not until thirty years later, in 1984, at age thirty-six, in my fifteenth year of teaching that I first heard the words *Tourette Syndrome*. It was my good fortune to be watching an episode of *Quincy, M.E.*, on television one Sunday night as I worked on lesson plans for the upcoming week. The subject of that episode of *Quincy* was Tourette Syndrome. It was a night that changed my life forever.

At the end of the program, the station listed the name, address, and phone number of the national Tourette Syndrome Association (TSA). As you can imagine, I was calling that number the very next morning, even before I started my homeroom. TSA sent me two brochures about TS and the physicians' referral list for the state of New York, where I reside. Sadly, twenty-five years ago, there were only two names on that list. The closest doctor to me was one and a half hours away, and I immediately called him and made an appointment. He was so busy that he couldn't see me for over three months. It was during that appointment, three months after seeing the *Quincy* episode, that I was officially diagnosed with TS and obsessive-compulsive disorder (OCD). I remember that day very well, because I cried most of the way home from that appointment. Those were cathartic tears, for all that I and my whole family had been through.

What I didn't know when I watched that episode of *Quincy* was that TS and OCD are hereditary disorders, and during those three months I came to the realization that my whole family had these disorders. I had five brothers and sisters, and they all had TS, as did many other family members—including my sixty-three-year-old mother—but none of them had ever been diagnosed. My mind reeled, thinking how different things might have been for all of us if we had been diagnosed in childhood and received help early on.

Within a few months I decided to start a TSA chapter in my part of the state. We needed only seven signatures on a petition to become a chapter, but because TS was considered a very rare disorder, it was harder than you might imagine gathering those seven signatures. I did succeed and was able to start a TSA chapter with six other dedicated volunteers. Twenty-five years later we are still going strong and have a mailing list of hundreds of families across the state of New York. What I originally believed—that TS was a very rare disorder—has proven not to be true. We now know that between one in two hundred and one in eight hundred people have TS. At a recent teacher in-service training I led at a small private high school, there were four children diagnosed with TS in that school alone. I tell educational personnel all the time that the chance of them encountering a child with TS in the course of their career is 100 percent.

## We've Come a Long Way—or Have We?

When I began my teaching career in 1969, my annual salary was $6,800, female teachers were not allowed to wear pants to school, we copied written work on a mimeograph machine, and students with "special needs" were locked away in a room with the windows covered. They were feared by teachers and other students. VCRs (not to mention DVD players) had not been invented, computers were nonexistent, pocket calculators cost $50, and ADHD was referred to as "minimal brain dysfunction."

When I retired in 2002, VCRs, DVD players, Smart Boards, and computers had become integral parts of my classroom, and at least one-fourth of the students that I taught in the course of each day in my general education classroom had special needs. I had finally been diagnosed with TS and OCD, and I am also happy to report that my salary had increased considerably.

This is called progress. It was not easy for a "slightly older" teacher who was somewhat set in her ways to learn how to operate a computer, program a VCR, and integrate these media into her daily classroom instruction. But what choice did I have? The task of accepting children with special needs into my classroom was even more daunting. In fact, it was downright scary. We had not been prepared to teach these children. Teacher training had not kept up with federal regulations and new educational trends. And the most difficult task was to change the way I looked at kids with special needs. We have always been taught that if it quacks and waddles, it's a duck. So when a child makes noises in your class, comes to class without necessary supplies, or shouts out without raising his hand, then he must be a willfully disruptive, irresponsible, or unmotivated child.

We have readily accepted progress in the fields of science, technology, and medical research. We have encouraged it, applauded it, and at times even contributed to it. Those of us in the education field pride ourselves on keeping up with the latest pedagogic methodology. Yet we still often struggle with things that quack and waddle but are not ducks. In other words, we still unfairly judge children by their "quacks and waddles," most especially those with neurological disorders. We often still use methods of discipline with these children that we used thirty years ago—punishing them for perceived "willful disruption," instead of treating them with understanding and compassion as children with a disability.

The difference now is that research and experience have made the knowledge and the resources available to us as educators to help us better understand the complexities of TS. When a child makes noises in class, when a child can't sit still, when a child forgets her pencil, this child may not be a duck at all. She may very well be a child with TS and ADHD or other neurological disorders that affect brain chemistry and cause some kids to behave differently from other kids.

Children don't die from TS, but their spirit dies a little each and every day as they go out and try to make their way in a world that doesn't understand them. It is my hope that this book will change the way we all look at children with neurological disorders and will help parents and teachers to better understand TS, OCD, and all of the associated disorders, so that the spirits of these children can live on.

# Introduction

Tourette Syndrome (TS) and obsessive-compulsive disorder (OCD) are two of the most widely misdiagnosed and misunderstood neurological disorders affecting children's educational performance and social and emotional well-being today. Thankfully, most educators have at least heard about TS and OCD. However, despite the significant media attention that TS and OCD receive, most people still know very little about them, and what they do know is often inaccurate.

There is a mystique about TS, a perplexity that often aligns it with bad behavior. OCD can be even more difficult to understand because it is often hidden, unlike motor and vocal tics; it may look instead like a child exhibiting bizarre behaviors or an obstinate and defiant student. If OCD and TS are treated as such in a classroom setting, no one wins—not the teacher, not the administration, and, most important, not the child. These disorders are easiest to understand when we view them as the medical conditions they are, just as we view the other medical conditions that teachers deal with every day in their classrooms.

We would never think of punishing a child who was exhibiting the confusion and out-of-sorts behavior associated with low blood sugar in diabetes. No teacher would ever reprimand a child who is disrupting the class with an asthma attack or an epileptic seizure. Yet a student exhibiting the motor and vocal tics associated with TS or the peculiar behaviors of OCD is often disciplined for symptoms of this medical, neurological disorder, to his or her extreme embarrassment and distress. Why does this happen? It happens because people understand diabetes and asthma, whereas most people misinterpret TS and OCD.

I have worked with thousands of children with TS and/or OCD over the past twenty-five years through my work with the Greater New York State Chapter of the Tourette Syndrome Association, my position on the national TSA board, and as the education specialist for TSA. I want to thank these wonderful children in advance for not only all that they have taught me but also for allowing me to use them as (unnamed) examples throughout this book, so that others can better understand this most baffling disorder and the individuals who live with it.

> One of the most successful coping mechanisms I have developed over the years I have lived with TS is my sense of humor. It has helped me survive this disorder and defuse many a difficult or embarrassing situation. You will undoubtedly detect this propensity as you read ahead. I am in no way making light of this very difficult disorder or the pain that people with TS suffer across their lifetimes. It is simply my way of managing life with TS.

# Section One

## BASIC INFORMATION ABOUT TS, OCD, AND ASSOCIATED DISORDERS

1.1.   What Is Tourette Syndrome (TS)?

1.2.   Manifestations of Motor Tics

1.3.   Manifestations of Vocal Tics

1.4.   Waxing and Waning of Symptoms

1.5.   Suppression of Symptoms

1.6.   Other Related Tic Disorders

1.7.   Medical Treatment of TS

1.8.   Associated Disorders

1.9.   What Is Attention Deficit Hyperactivity Disorder (ADHD)?

1.10.  Dysgraphia

1.11.  Executive Dysfunction

1.12.  Depression

1.13.  Sleep Disorders

1.14.  Sensory Processing

1.15.  Learning Disabilities

1.16.  Auditory Processing Difficulties

1.17.  Social Skills Deficits

1.18.  Behavioral Issues

1.19.  What Is Obsessive-Compulsive Disorder (OCD)?

1.20. Manifestations of OCD

1.21. Medical Treatments for OCD

1.22. Behavioral Interventions for OCD

## 1.1. What Is Tourette Syndrome (TS)?

- Tourette Syndrome (TS; sometimes also known as Tourette's Disorder) is a complex neurobiological movement disorder resulting from a chemical imbalance in the brain.
- It is characterized by involuntary movements and vocalizations referred to as motor and vocal tics.
- TS occurs three to four times more frequently in boys than girls.
- At present there is no cure for TS.
- TS is hereditary.
- TS is not a degenerative disorder and does not get progressively worse.
- Several genes most likely cause TS, and to date only one has been identified. The genetic basis of tic disorders and TS is currently being intensely studied.
- There is currently no medical test that will clinically diagnose TS.

Although it is well documented that TS is a neurological disorder, onlookers sometimes mistakenly believe that TS symptoms are intentional behaviors.

- Tourette symptoms are sometimes misinterpreted as emotional, psychiatric, or behavioral problems. At school, children may be reprimanded and punished for their symptoms, and some are even asked not to return to school.

As with Parkinson's disease, dopamine, a brain chemical involved with movement, is believed to be prominently involved in Tourette Syndrome. (But having TS does not mean that the patient will develop Parkinson's.)

- With Parkinson's, the brain is no longer producing enough dopamine, so people with Parkinson's exhibit slowed-down movements such as tremors, slurred speech, and muscle rigidity.

- Because of the involvement of dopamine and the involuntary movements and vocalizations that people with TS exhibit, TS can be easily seen as truly neurological. (Again I emphasize that TS does not lead to Parkinson's.)
- Because there is currently no medical test to diagnose TS, it is identified by the presence of these five observable diagnostic criteria:
  - Multiple motor tics
  - At least one vocal tic
  - Waxing and waning of symptoms
  - Childhood onset of symptoms
  - Symptoms lasting for at least one year

Although educators cannot formally diagnose TS, it is extremely important for them to know where the diagnosis comes from, what they are looking for, and what they may see with a child with whom they are working who has TS.

- Educators can be key in helping to identify a child with TS.
- They can often be a resource to the family by providing them with TS literature and by helping them to locate a knowledge-able physician in their area to obtain a proper diagnosis.

## 1.2. Manifestations of Motor Tics

A motor tic is defined as a rapid, repetitive movement of any voluntary muscular group in your body. There are two categories of motor tics: simple and complex.

- Simple motor tics are the easiest to recognize because they look like tics. They affect just one muscular group.
- Over the years people have referred to these movements as twitches or nervous habits, thus equating them with a psychological problem. The official term for them is *tics.*
- Simple motor tics rarely interrupt a classroom, so they often go unnoticed by teachers. *Simple motor tics* include:
  - Rapid eye blinking
  - Head jerking
  - Facial grimaces
  - Arm flailing
  - Finger tapping
  - Neck twisting
  - Nose twitching
  - Hand and finger movements
  - Lip smacking
  - Leg jerks
  - Hair tossing
- Although these simple movements may not disturb other students, they can be very interfering to the child who has TS.
- Imagine constantly shaking your head back and forth and trying to read or twisting your wrists over and over again and trying to write.
- These tics can occur in bouts that sometimes seem purposeful, and children are sometimes unjustly accused of performing their tics to get attention or to get a laugh from other students.

- *Complex motor tics* are intricate and complicated movements, and the list of them is seemingly endless. Almost any simple or complex movement can be a motor tic.
- These complex movements involve more than one muscular group and don't always look like what most people would define as a tic.
- These tics are the most difficult to recognize and the most misunderstood. Examples of *complex motor tics* are:
  - Hopping
  - Knee bending
  - Whole body bending
  - Twirling
  - Clapping
  - Touching objects and/or other people
  - Obscene gestures
  - Stomach crunching
  - A series of what look like simple motor tics
  - Self-abusive tics such as hitting oneself in the head or hitting one's leg against a desk
  - Handstands and cartwheels

See the Appendix at the end of the book for many more examples of complex motor tics.

## 1.3. Manifestations of Vocal Tics

- Vocal tics can often be the most problematic type of tic. They are called vocal tics because you hear them. A vocal tic can be defined as follows:
  - The repeated uttering of a sound, word, or phrase
  - A noise that someone makes over and over again
  - A change in speech pattern or voice inflection, stuttering, or speaking with an accent
- Vocal tics, like motor tics, are divided into *simple* and *complex* types. Simple vocal tics involve noisemaking, while complex vocal tics are usually something linguistically meaningful that a person says—a word, a phrase, a complete sentence, or an atypical speech pattern.
- Examples of *simple vocal tics* are:
  - Constant sniffing
  - Throat clearing
  - A squeaking sound
  - Snorting
  - Howling
  - Barking
  - Grunting
  - Humming
  - Hissing
  - Screeching
  - Sighing
  - Coughing
- Examples of *complex vocal tics* are:
  - Vocal repetition of a phrase or word. (One of my favorites was a boy who would repeat, "chickens are fuzzy, chickens are fuzzy" and "I have a chicken in my pants.")

- Changes in tone or volume of speech in the middle of a sentence
- Stuttering
- The urge to speak in a foreign accent
- Speaking in a baby voice

The three very complex vocal tics can seem quite strange to those hearing them for the first time:

- *Echolalia*: the repeating of someone else's words or words one has picked up from television or the radio (such as "Can you hear me now?" or "Afflac!").
- *Pallilalia*: the repetition of one's own words. (One child needed to say hello to his teacher each morning in eight different tones of voice. If he was interrupted, he had to start all over again.)
- *Coprolalia*: the involuntary uttering of anything inappropriate, from cursing to ethnic slurs, negative comments about a person's appearance, or even sexual comments (such as "dumb ass," "you're fat," or "I had sex last night").
  - Coprolalia can certainly be a part of Tourette, but it is *not* necessary for a diagnosis.
  - Coprolalia occurs very infrequently—in only about 15 percent of people with TS—but is often the most problematic of all tics.
- Many people are under the impression that such inappropriate words are uttered randomly, but this is not necessarily the case.
  - People with TS can be very suggestible; they may be reacting to something or someone they have seen or heard (as when a child sees someone wearing a revealing outfit and has to shout out "Whore").
  - The inappropriate words can be completely random, but they can also be triggered just as easily by someone or something that one sees. (See the Appendix for many more examples of this phenomenon.)

- Vocal tics, like all tics, are a result of an imbalance of brain chemicals, and they sometimes affect the person's ability to inhibit behavior. This tendency is similar to some people's experience after a stroke or a traumatic brain injury: they suddenly become disinhibited while the brain is healing. People understand the trauma situation because they can see that the brain has been damaged, but with TS, that's just how the brain functions day to day.

- TS has often been referred to as a disability of disinhibition.

## 1.4. Waxing and Waning of Symptoms

The third criterion for a diagnosis of TS is the *waxing and waning of symptoms*. This criterion has two implications.

- The first implication is that tics naturally change all the time.
    - You could be teaching a child who has a snorting tic and in a few weeks that tic could disappear and he could instead be shouting a word across your classroom.
    - Tics change much more frequently in children than adults, which makes this particular criterion one of the most difficult for educators to comprehend.
    - You just get used to one set of symptoms, and suddenly a new tic appears and replaces an old one. Sometimes the old ones don't disappear, but new ones are simply added on.
    - Typically tics tend to worsen right before puberty and improve in adolescence. There probably couldn't be a worse time in a person's life for this change to happen.
    - TS is very difficult socially, and most peers simply do not understand it.
- Waxing and waning also mean that tics change in severity depending on environmental factors. The most common of these are:
    - Stress
    - Anxiety
    - Excitement
    - Fatigue
    - Illness
- Testing situations can be very stressful and are also the time when the classroom is most quiet, which makes vocal tics especially problematic for children with TS.
- Events such as family birthdays, vacations, and field trips can be very exciting for a child, which could temporarily cause symptoms to worsen.

- Tics almost always tend to worsen at the end of the day because of the level of fatigue.
- Overheating of the body can cause an increase in tics for some children.

### Childhood Onset

- TS is a disorder of childhood onset. It first manifests itself anywhere between the ages of two and eighteen.
- The most common age of onset of symptoms is six or seven.
- The first tics to appear are commonly facial tics of some sort.

(My first tic at age six was eye blinking. Since no one had any idea why I was doing this, it was suggested that my mother take me to the eye doctor. I grew up in a very small town with very few medical options. The only optometrist in town prescribed bifocals for me at age six. To this day I call them my Tourette glasses. A few years later my brother got his Tourette glasses from the same doctor.)

## 1.5. Suppression of Symptoms

The suppression of symptoms may sound counterintuitive: although tics are involuntary, a person with TS does have the ability to suppress symptoms for very short amounts of time. This can be compared to trying to hold in a sneeze. One can do it for a short time, but the sneeze will eventually happen and will be much louder if you try to suppress it. Another analogy that might help you understand these phenomena is trying not to blink.

- Try not to blink your eyes for fifteen seconds. Some people can't do this at all, and for those who can it takes tremendous effort and concentration.
- As soon as the fifteen seconds are up, those who have succeeded will invariably begin to blink rapidly.
- If someone had continued to lecture to you while you were trying not to blink, could you listen attentively to what was being taught? The response is always no: you would be focused on trying not to blink.
- Holding in tics is never a good thing to ask a student to do: the tics become worse and the student will not be able to concentrate on anything but holding in his tics.
- Suppressing tics produces a great deal of anxiety.
- People try to suppress despite these undesirable consequences because ticking can be embarrassing and disruptive.
  - People with TS are frequently teased, made fun of, imitated, and even feared because of the strangeness of their symptoms.
  - People with TS will do anything to avoid these reactions.
  - Many students will simply become the "class clown," pretending to tic on purpose to avoid the teasing. (A middle school student once related that in school there was a club for bad but there was no club for weird, so he often pretended to do his tics on purpose to "be bad.")

Understanding TS is the first step to dealing with it appropriately in a classroom setting. When I speak to educators about TS, my first piece of advice is to be creative. Several chapters in this book will discuss the impact of TS and OCD on classroom performance and offer a plethora of strategies, techniques, and accommodations that will allow these kids to remain in a school setting, be understood, and be academically and socially successful.

## 1.6. Other Related Tic Disorders

It is important to note two milder tic disorders that are related to TS but are not full-blown Tourette Syndrome:

- Transient tic disorder
- Chronic motor or vocal tic disorder

### Transient Tics

- It is estimated that as many as one in ten children will develop a transient simple motor or vocal tic at some point during their school years.
- Such tics usually occur in just one muscle group and *last no more than a few months.*
- Doctors will not give a diagnosis of TS until the symptoms have existed for at least a year because of the high prevalence of transient tics in childhood.
- Transient tics may become more prominent when a child is stressed, tired, or excited.
- You will very likely see more than one child in your class experiencing a transient tic disorder.
  - The tic develops quickly.
  - It lasts for only a few weeks or a few months.
  - The tic will disappear just as quickly, never to be seen again.
  - This is a transient tic and is quite common.
- The prevalence of transient tic disorder is the reason for the fifth diagnostic criterion for TS—symptoms lasting longer than one year. Doctors want to be sure these symptoms are not just transient tics of childhood.

### Chronic Motor or Vocal Tic Disorder

- A chronic motor or vocal tic disorder manifests itself as one or two tics that start in childhood, never change, and never go away. These tics may change in frequency and intensity over time.

- A chronic tic disorder is probably the manifestation of the TS gene. It is not at all uncommon for a family member of someone with TS to have a chronic tic disorder.

- Think about a person you know or have encountered who has a constant sniffing, head jerk, eye blink, or some other single tic.
  - They always have it and it never changes.
  - We tend to get used to such phenomena in people we know well, and we usually stop noticing the tic.
  - These phenomena could be a chronic tic disorder.

## 1.7. Medical Treatment of TS

The medical treatment of TS is a very complex matter. When I was first diagnosed twenty-five years ago, only one medication was used to treat the tics of TS, and that was haloperidol (Haldol).

- Haloperidol is a very powerful neuroleptic medication. (A neuroleptic is a drug used in the treatment of neurological conditions that has a tranquilizing effect by reducing nerve activity.)
- When used for TS, haloperidol is prescribed in much smaller doses than it would be for a patient with a psychotic disorder.
- Many doctors will now initially prescribe either clonidine (Catapres) or guanfacine (Tenex), both antihypertensive medications, which have helped some patients and have far fewer side effects. These drugs are traditionally not as effective for suppressing tics as the neuroleptics.
- Pharmaceutical research has since produced many other medications that are now used to treat TS. Many of these are in the same family as haloperidol.
  - There is considerable argument about whether the "newer" neuroleptic medications have fewer neurological side effects.
  - These medications will reduce tics, but none is a cure. There are no medications that will immediately, completely, and permanently eliminate tics.
- A few other medications in the neuroleptic group of drugs that have a similar effect on tics are:
  - Pimozide (Orap©)
  - Risperidone (Risperdal©)
  - Olanzapine (Zyprexia©)
  - Ziprasidone (Geodon©)
  - Aripiprazole (Abilify©)
- Response to any of these drugs can vary widely from patient to patient.

- Medication treatment of tic disorders can be complicated and should always be supervised by a physician experienced in the management of these disorders.

- Extreme patience is required of everyone concerned as the medication is introduced and the dose adjusted.

- New medications are always being studied. Nonetheless, many of these can still produce unpleasant side effects such as:
  - Depression
  - Significant weight gain
  - Glucose intolerance
  - Increased irritability
  - Lethargy
  - Fatigue
  - Cognitive dulling
  - Increased aggression

- Comprehensive Behavioral Intervention for Tics (CBIT) is a relatively new treatment for tics. A DVD on CBIT is available from TSA (www.tsa-usa.org).

- Each person is an individual and can react quite differently from others to a medication.
  - It is always the parents' decision whether to medicate their children.
  - Some choose not to medicate because of unwanted side effects.

- Some families turn to more natural approaches to treating the disorder involving diet, nutritional supplements (which are not regulated by any agency, may contain additional ingredients not listed on the label, and ingredients may not be correct amounts), environment, exercise, relaxation techniques, and so on.

- TS rarely exists alone. (This critical point will be discussed further in upcoming chapters.)

- TS is frequently accompanied by other neurological disorders.
- These associated disorders may need to be treated with completely different classes of medications.
- Physicians' referral lists for all states in the United States are available through the Tourette Syndrome Association (www.tsa-usa.org) and other state TS and OCD agencies.

## 1.8. Associated Disorders

Up to now we have looked at the five criteria necessary for a diagnosis of TS, but this discussion is just the tip of the iceberg for TS. TS is a neurological disorder, and as such it is almost always accompanied by other neurological and neuropsychiatric disorders.

The most common of these disorders are:

- Attention deficit hyperactivity disorder (ADHD)
- Obsessive-compulsive disorder (OCD)
- Learning disabilities (LD)
- Other common disorders and issues often coexisting with TS are:
  - Executive dysfunction (see List 1.11 later in this section for full definition)
  - Depression
  - Anxiety disorders
  - Sleep disorders
  - Fine motor skill difficulties (dysgraphia; see List 1.10 for full definition)
  - Sensory defensiveness (see List 1.14 for full definition)
  - Social skills deficits
  - Behavioral issues
  - Repeated anger-generated episodes (RAGE)
- Any of these disorders can exist alone without the others, but it is also extremely common to see these disorders in combination.
- Although the autism spectrum is considered a separate range of neurological disorders from TS, significant overlaps are increasingly appearing between these spectrums. The autism spectrum includes full-blown autism, Asperger syndrome, and pervasive developmental disorder.

## 1.9. What Is Attention Deficit Hyperactivity Disorder (ADHD)?

Jossey-Bass has published numerous books on attention deficit hyperactivity disorder (ADHD), so I will not duplicate the wonderful work of other authors on that topic here. I do, however, feel it is extremely important to discuss the relationship between TS and ADHD and how this complicates the lives of the numerous children who have both disorders.

- More than 50 percent of persons with TS also have ADHD, which can often be the precursor to TS.
- ADHD appears within the first few years of life, and the tics usually start around the age of five or six.
- ADHD is characterized by several symptoms, which include:

### 1. Inattentiveness

- Easily distracted by even the smallest extraneous noise
- Difficulty sustaining attention
- Difficulty staying on task

### 2. Impulsiveness

- Blurting out comments without being called on
- Failing to think before acting
- Doing dangerous things without thinking of consequences
- Difficulty regulating emotional responses to situations

### 3. Hyperactivity

- Nervous system is understimulated
- Inability to sit still for long periods of time
- Needing constant movement: finger tapping, chewing gum, and so on
- Concentrating better when they are making some movement

### 4. Disorganization

- Difficulty with tasks requiring organization, memory, and time management; this symptom is also known as executive dysfunction. (See List 1.11 for in-depth discussion of executive dysfunction.)

### 5. Socially Immaturity

- Social-emotional age is often about two-thirds of their chronological age
- Difficulty in social interactions with children their own age
- Preferring to play with younger children
- Often responding in a manner that is not age-appropriate

In the classroom, ADHD children can display several behaviors:

- Are very fidgety
- Have a difficult time remaining seated for any length of time
- Seem to be in constant motion
- Have a very short attention span
- Get in your face and shout out answers before being called on
- Have a difficult time initiating or finishing any task
- Are some of the most disorganized children you will ever encounter
- Always come to your class unprepared and with the wrong materials
- Lose everything—pencils, pens, paper, and homework

Children with ADHD can be some of the most frustrating children you will ever teach. Although it is initially tempting for us as educators to view this disorder as simply bad behavior, that couldn't be further from reality. Medications traditionally used to treat ADHD are stimulants, and these medications may exacerbate the tics and/or the OCD. *A certain number of children with TS are able to take stimulants without significant increases in tic activity, but many cannot.*

## 1.10. Dysgraphia

Dysgraphia is a specific learning disability that affects how easily children acquire written language and how well they use written language to express their thoughts. It affects an extremely large number of children with TS and/or ADHD.

- Many people with dysgraphia have gone undiagnosed their whole lives.
- Dysgraphia can be the result of fine motor skills weakness, and/or a disconnect between what the mind sees and what is actually produced on paper.
- Dysgraphia is one of the primary reasons why affected children become frustrated, refuse to do their work, and ultimately fail. When you can't write, you can't do your work: it's as simple as that.
- Characteristics of dysgraphia can include:
  - Slow and laborious writing
  - Hand and finger cramping
  - Letter reversal ("d" becomes a "b")
  - Letter reversals within a word ("read" becomes "raed")
  - Sloppy handwriting, uneven spacing, irregular margins, and inconsistent lettering
  - Inability to copy correctly from book to paper or chalkboard to paper (poor visual-motor skills)
  - Difficulty with written expression: getting thoughts onto paper
  - Difficulty with punctuation and capitalization
  - Difficulty with note taking
  - Poor spelling
- In addition to these characteristics, we also add interfering tics, obsessions, and sensory issues that interfere with writing

for children with TS and OCD. Handwriting can be extremely difficult, if not impossible, for these children.

- These children will be seen writing a few words, then stopping and shaking out their hand before they can continue—it actually hurts to write.

- The more they write, the more it hurts and the more fatigued their hand becomes, which results in completely illegible work and increased frustration.

- There are times when a child can write a few sentences without too much trouble, but that ability waxes and wanes just like the tics.

- Any hand, finger, eye, or upper-body tic can interfere with the writing process.

- Obsessions such as writing and erasing words until they look perfect can also hinder writing.

- Some children with sensory issues may have a difficult time touching certain types of paper.

- Children who exhibit signs of dysgraphia should be evaluated by an occupational therapist, who can identify this disability and provide therapy as well as useful accommodations.

- When occupational therapists test these children, they *must*:

  - Give them a writing sample that is long enough to reveal a wide array of possible writing difficulties.

  - Test them under less-than-optimum conditions that mimic what they would normally be doing in a classroom setting.

  - Collect a large sampling of their everyday written work to conduct a more accurate evaluation.

  - Look for interfering tics, obsessions, writing rituals, and so on.

- Following are common classroom difficulties for children with dysgraphia:

  - Numbers may be reversed when students are copying math problems from the textbook to note paper.

- Numbers may be lined up incorrectly (for example, the tens column may be lined up with the hundreds column), resulting in a wrong answer.
- Homework assignments may be copied incorrectly from the board.
- Individual letters and letters within a word may be reversed.
- Cursive writing may be an impossible skill to acquire.
- A child can know very well how to spell a word verbally, but when she writes it she reverses letters.
- Taking notes may be impossible.

Children with dysgraphia may be very creative writers, yet they continually write the shortest amount possible. This is not because they are lazy, but because it hurts too much to write anything longer and it will invariably be illegible. This disability can be easily accommodated, but it must first be recognized as a disability and not misinterpreted as lazy or oppositional behavior.

# 1.11. Executive Dysfunction

Executive functioning refers to the mental processes involved in goal-directed activity. Executive functions most directly related to academic performance include:

- Setting goals
- Making a plan to accomplish a task
- Keeping the plan in one's working memory while executing it
- Sequencing the steps in the plan
- Initiating those steps and shifting from one to another
- Monitoring one's progress
- Regulating one's attention and emotional responses to challenges that arise
- Being flexible in changing the plan if necessary
- Evaluating the plan for possible use in a subsequent similar activity

In a classroom setting, these challenges translate to a child who will have great difficulty:

- Keeping track of his belongings
- Organizing her materials
- Getting started on a task and staying on task
- Breaking down long assignments or projects into smaller tasks
- Sequencing information
- Forming goals
- Writing down homework assignments
- Managing his time
- Performing to her potential

Children with executive function problems will likely:

- Lose their homework and other materials
- Come to class unprepared

- Have a disorganized desk and locker
- Fail to finish anything
- Have difficulty managing workload
- Become quickly overwhelmed

## 1.12. Depression

- Depression is unfortunately often difficult to detect in children.
- Depressed children may not exhibit the same traits and behaviors as depressed adults.
- Depressed children often become increasingly oppositional, aggressive and defiant and begin to act out.
- Depression is not uncommon in children with these disorders and must be assessed and treated by a qualified physician.

## 1.13. Sleep Disorders

Children with TS and OCD can experience a number of sleep disorders. Rarely will teachers know that the problems they are seeing in the classroom result from sleep problems: what they see is a tired, cranky, out-of-sorts child. Children with sleep disorders will have a difficult time functioning and performing to their potential in the classroom. Sleep disorders related to TS and OCD may include:

- Insomnia
- Restless sleep
- Night terrors
- Difficulty waking up
- Very deep sleep
- Walking or talking in one's sleep

# 1.14. Sensory Processing

Sensory processing disorder is the constant bombardment of sensory input that is neither perceived nor interpreted correctly. It can affect any of the senses and cause great anxiety or pain for the child, as well as problems with:

- Daily functioning
- Family relationships
- Regulating emotions and behavior
- Self-esteem
- Learning and performance at school

In the course of a day children with sensory processing issues may vacillate between being hypersensitive and hyposensitive. They may be extremely sensitive to light touch, jerking away from a soft pat on the shoulder one moment, while at another time be seemingly indifferent to pain. When you see a child do the following things, you may be seeing red flags signaling *hyposensitivity*:

- Appear sluggish
- Have self-abusive behaviors, tics, or obsessions
- Pick at skin, scabs, or nails
- Repeatedly touch surfaces or objects that are soothing
- Crave strong sensory input

If you see a child doing these things, you may be seeing examples of sensory *hypersensitivity*:

- Is sensitive to sudden touch or the feel of certain fabrics
- Can't touch certain surfaces such as paper or a countertop
- Needs to have tags cut out of clothes or socks without seams
- Is very sensitive to bright or fluorescent lights

- Can't tolerate the texture of certain foods in her mouth
- Is very sensitive to certain smells
- Is overreactive to certain sounds
- Appears to hear everything at equally loud volume
- Melts down or becomes more aggressive in noisy chaotic environments where there is high sensory overload

When I visit a school to work with a child who has developed "behavioral" problems and I question teachers about where the behaviors most frequently occur, they often respond with:

- The hallways between classes
- The cafeteria
- The playground
- The school bus
- Physical education class
- School assemblies

These are all areas of high sensory overload, which may be intolerable to children with this disorder. The environment plays a huge role in the day-to-day functioning of these children. We need to consider making environmental accommodations to help meet their needs and eradicate certain behaviors that are caused by reactions to the environment.

## 1.15. Learning Disabilities

Learning disabilities affect the brain's ability to receive and process information and can make it problematic for a person to learn as quickly or in the same way as someone who isn't affected by a learning disability.

- A significant number of children with Tourette Syndrome also have learning disabilities.
- Virtually any learning disability can be present.
- A full battery of neuropsychological evaluations should be performed to help identify which learning disabilities are affecting the child.
- Very frequently these disabilities are found in the nonverbal areas.
- The most common of these, some of which have already been discussed, are:
  - Auditory processing difficulties
  - Dysgraphia
  - Executive dysfunction
  - Social skills deficits
- The learning disabilities are usually not directly related to the severity of the child's tics.
- Tics in themselves can be disruptive to the child's performance, as can the mental effort it takes to attempt to suppress tics. This ongoing effort can interfere with reading, handwriting, and attention, to name a few challenges.
- The other associated disorders of ADHD and OCD can also have a significant impact on attention, concentration and task completion.
- It is essential that these children receive appropriate testing, which should usually include occupational therapy and speech language evaluations, in light of the considerable number of children with TS who have deficits in these areas.

## 1.16. Auditory Processing Difficulties

Many children with TS and OCD have some difficulty processing spoken language. This difficulty could be a symptom of a true auditory processing disorder or it could be the result of what I call a "dysregulated auditory system." It can also mimic ADHD.

- Sensory issues, discussed earlier in this section, often affect auditory abilities, making it difficult for children to sift out noises and speech in the environment.
- Affected children seem to hear everything at the same volume, which makes them very distractible.
- Background noises are very distracting for these students, even when they are at a very low volume.

It is always a good idea to have the child tested by a speech language pathologist or possibly even an audiologist to help sort out what is really going on. Regardless of what the issue is, the results often look the same and cause the same difficulties for a child:

- Processing and following directions, both simple and complex
- Processing abstract information (math word problems)
- Following conversations
- Performing well in noisy environments
- Processing spoken language quickly
- Remembering information such as directions or lists
- Hearing the difference between sounds or words that are similar
- Higher-level listening tasks
- Focusing

## 1.17. Social Skills Deficits

Many children with TS and associated disorders exhibit social skills deficits similar to children on the autism spectrum. Children with social skills issues will have difficulty with the following:

- Interacting with peers
- Understanding social "rules"
- Establishing eye contact
- Understanding social nuances and picking up on social cues
- Perceiving the feelings of others
- Understanding pragmatic language (saying inappropriate or unrelated things during conversations, telling stories in a disorganized way, having little variety in language use)

They will tend to:

- Interact normally with adults, but not with their peers
- Experience social anxiety
- Prefer activities they can do alone
- Demonstrate lack of judgment
- Experience social rejection
- Play with children much younger than they are
- Be able to *explain* what they need to do in social situations, but unable to *demonstrate* it in real-life situations

## 1.18. Behavioral Issues

Children on the TS and OCD spectrum of neurological disorders are often prone to difficult behaviors. These behaviors can include:

- Bouts of crying
- Inappropriate responses or overreactions to situations
- Tantrums (RAGE)
- Throwing things
- Complete meltdowns or rage attacks
- Impulsive behaviors

Although these behaviors may look like those of a spoiled, defiant, and undisciplined child, they are decidedly not. These behaviors are almost always triggered by some aspect of the child's neurological disorders.

It is up to the parents and professionals to figure out what is causing these behaviors and implement environmental accommodations and specific strategies to help eliminate these incidences. Sections Three and Four of this book have behavioral assessments that have been created specifically to work with these children. It is critical that everyone working with these children understand why the behavior occurs. As an analogy, consider the following scenario:

- Most of us start each weekday with the ringing of an alarm.
- Some days we push the snooze button two or three times before waking up enough to get out of bed.
- Once we have finally arisen, had coffee, showered, and had breakfast, we are usually in an optimum mood to face the responsibilities of the day and be nice to our family members and co-workers.
- In only a handful of times in the course of our lives will we find ourselves in a state of mind where we say and do extreme

things that we normally never say or do. We often don't even remember that we have said or done such things. Examples of these situations are:

- A traumatic incident
- A car accident
- Sudden hospitalization of a loved one
- A house fire
- Sudden death of a loved one
- Loss of a job

- In any of these cases we may say or do things that are completely out of character. We might swear at a police officer, scream at a loved one, or throw something.

- People almost always understand this type of reaction in light of the exceptional circumstances and usually forgive us for our words and actions.

- We almost always feel terrible and apologize. Fortunately, this only happens a few times in a lifetime.

- Children with these disorders can go *unpredictably* in and out of this "zone" several times a day. They may say inappropriate things, push other children, scream at their mother or teacher, or go into a full-blown meltdown for what appears to most people to be absolutely no reason.

- If we analyze these behavioral episodes using the assessments provided, we will quickly see a pattern developing that will lead us to the actual trigger of the behavior.

- The most common precipitating factors of such behavioral episodes are:

  - Sensory overload in noisy, chaotic environments
  - Getting stuck (for children with OCD)
  - Fatigue (from medications or lack of sleep)
  - Teasing
  - Inability to write

- Anxiety or obsessive fears
- Feeling of being overwhelmed by a long assignment or several assignments

Consider, for example, a child with sensory issues in the tactile area who maneuvers through his day as if he had the worst sunburn of his life and his mother made him wear a wool sweater over the sunburn. If someone simply bumps into him in the hallway, his immediate reaction might be to hit that other student because bumping into someone with a wool sweater over a sunburn hurts. But to the onlooker, this appears to be an extreme overreaction to any everyday occurrence.

- It is up to the adults working with the affected child to look at the behavior and the precipitating factors and help change the child's environment and/or give her compensatory strategies that will prevent the behavior from recurring.
- Children who demonstrate such over-the-top behaviors always feel badly afterward for what they have done. They simply can't stop themselves.

## 1.19. What Is Obsessive-Compulsive Disorder (OCD)?

In my opinion, obsessive-compulsive disorder (OCD) may be the most closely related disorder to the tics of TS. I often refer to obsessions and compulsions as "tics of the mind." As the body ticks, the mind also ticks, as it gets "stuck" on thoughts and ideas—the difference is that obsessions are not usually as apparent to onlookers as tics.

- An obsession is an intrusive and recurring thought, image, or impulse that your mind gets stuck on which is unpleasant and disrupts functioning.
- Compulsions are behaviors that are used to reduce the anxiety accompanying the obsessions.
- It is often difficult to separate obsessions from compulsions.
- OCD also shares the chronic waxing and waning traits of TS.
  - The tics and the obsessions change frequently.
  - Obsessions and compulsions are exacerbated by stress, excitement, and fatigue, as are the tics of TS.

## 1.20. Manifestations of OCD

OCD has an enormous number of manifestations. Each person you encounter will be different and may experience a variety of obsessions and compulsions that can change over the course of his lifetime. Some of the most common OCD traits are:

- The need for symmetry, perfection, and neatness
- Repeated counting
- Checking things over and over
- Constant doubt or worrying
- Obsessive fears
- Fear of germs and contamination
- Ritualistic behaviors
- Asking questions repeatedly
- Difficulty with transitions or any kind of change or inflexibility
- An obsessive sense of justice
- Obsessive thoughts

OCD almost always appears irrational to the onlooker and often even to the person who has it, but despite the absurdity of these obsessions and compulsions, the affected person cannot stop. Children with OCD are often referred to as obstinate or oppositional because they get stuck and can't move on. One young child taught me a great analogy for this tendency: she likened her OCD to a hamster on a wheel. The wheel keeps going round and round and you can't get off.

Below are specific examples of common OCD traits and how they may manifest in a child with this disorder. Parents and educators need to learn to look for these "red flags" for OCD.

*Symmetry, Perfectionism, and Neatness*

- Pencils, pens, and books must be lined up perfectly.
- Window blinds must be precisely symmetrical.

- The bedspread cannot have any wrinkles and must hang evenly on all sides of the bed.
- Words must be written and erased over and over again until they look perfect.
- Pencils must be sharpened repeatedly as the lead wears down even slightly.
- Clothes in the closet must be hung by color.
- Homework must be copied over and over until it appears perfect; even the shortest assignment takes hours to accomplish.
- On tests that require bubbling answers on a separate sheet, the bubble must be filled in flawlessly.

### Counting Obsessions

- A person can become obsessed with counting things over and over again. This practice goes on inside her head, so no one ever sees it happening.
- People with OCD always doubt that they did something right the first time, so they must do it repeatedly, just to be sure.
- People with this obsession may find it necessary to count:
  - Stairs as they climb them
  - Ceiling tiles
  - Chairs in a classroom
  - Words as they read or write
- This counting takes endless amounts of time, impedes concentration, and interferes with the task to be accomplished.

### Checking Things Over and Over

- Everyone tends to check things, but the person without OCD can check once or twice and be done. The person with true OCD cannot stop checking.

- People with OCD may have to check the stove, the coffeepot, the iron, and the thermostat eight or nine times before they can leave their house.
- A student could become stuck checking the combination lock on his locker.
- Students may have to check their work over and over again; they are often the last ones to turn in their tests.
- Some people with OCD spend an inordinate amount of time with bedtime rituals such as:
  - Checking all the door locks several times
  - Checking to make sure all the lights are off
  - Making sure the alarm clock is set properly
  - Saying goodnight to people several times

### Constant Doubt and Worrying: Generalized Anxiety

- Kids who struggle with doubt and worry often look like kids who are just trying to get out of attending school or doing their work.
- The worry sometimes seems to come out of nowhere, with no precipitating incident.
- It can take the form of irrational fears that start suddenly.
  - A child may be unable to attend school or go into a certain class for a long period of time.
  - A student may have to call home several times a day to ensure that everyone is OK.
  - Some may have to always sit near the classroom door or carry a cell phone in their pocket for extra assurance.

### Obsessive Fears

- Obsessive fears may be precipitated by an event or simply come out of nowhere.
  - A child may suddenly become terrified of fire and be unable to stay in the kitchen when her mother is cooking or is terrified by a fire drill at school.

- A child may suddenly become fearful of sleeping in his own bed or riding the school bus.

### Germs and Contamination

- One of the most common obsessions that we hear about is a germ obsession. Affected people have a fear of germs and contamination, most often irrational.
- To alleviate this obsession, these people must wash and/or avoid touching things that they believe to be contaminated. They may:
  - Wash their hands over and over again
  - Take very long and frequent showers
  - Clean their houses and belongings continually
  - Be unable to open doors without covering their hands
  - Be unable to use public restrooms at all
  - You can imagine the disruption this causes in someone's life. Some people have germ obsessions so severe that they cannot leave their homes. (One young boy had to wash his money to disinfect it before he was able to use it.)

### Ritualistic Behaviors

- Many people with OCD develop rituals that they have to complete over and over again. They may have to:
  - Touch certain things in a certain order
  - Back out of a room that they have walked into
  - Have their parents or teachers repeat something over and over again until it sounds just right to them
  - Keep pushing on a glass full of something until it spills

### Asking Repeated Questions

- At some point in her career, every teacher has encountered a student who asks constant questions. This is a huge red flag for OCD.
  - A child may ask the same question over and over again.

- There is a fear that they haven't received the correct information the first time and must keep asking.
- They may ask you to repeatedly check to make sure they have the correct homework assignment recorded or have the correct due date for a project.

### Difficulty with Transitions or Any Kind of Change

- Most children with OCD have difficulty with change.
- The change can be just a simple transition from one activity to another within a class or a major life adjustment such as changing schools or moving to a new city.
- These children are often referred to as stubborn or obstinate.
- They appear very inflexible, and any even minor changes in the day's schedule—what's for dinner or a cancelled play date—can cause them to melt down for lengthy periods of time.
- What looks like an insignificant incident to others may be more than the chronically inflexible child with OCD can cope with.
- This inflexibility can quickly turn into a "behavior" issue.
- Children with OCD may have a strong need to complete things:
  - If they are asked to put something away and start something new when the original task is not completed to their satisfaction, they become very irritable and oppositional.
  - They need transition warnings.
- A child may find it impossible to shift from one activity within a class period to another without a five-minute advance warning and repeated reminders every minute after that.
  - If the teacher simply says, "Put away your math homework and take out your spelling book," the math paper will invariably go flying across the room.
  - A "To Finish Later" basket can be created in the classroom where work that was not completed to a child's satisfaction can be placed. It may also be necessary to decide at that

moment exactly what time the child is going to come back and finish the work so that she can move on to the next activity.

### An Obsessive Sense of Justice

- Many people with OCD have what I call "an obsessive sense of justice." Red flags for this tendency in a classroom may include:
  - Tattle tales: children who must make sure that you know about every infraction of other children in the class
  - A child who debates every issue, from a grade on a test to a new rule
  - A child who is overly critical of other children if they don't measure up to his expectations

### Obsessive Thoughts

- Obsessive thoughts are words, songs, poems, or other thoughts that repeat over and over in one's head, sometimes for months at a time.
- These thoughts can be violent and create fear for the individual.

The items in this list are certainly not the only manifestations of OCD that you will ever see. Other less common OCD traits include:

- Hoarding
- Collecting things
- Pulling out one's hair (tricotillamania)
- Compulsive stealing (kleptomania)

## 1.21. Medical Treatments for OCD

For many years there was no medication available for the treatment of OCD. Several medications are now used, many of which are the same medications used for depression. Referred to as SSRIs (selective serotonin reuptake inhibitors), these medications include:

- Fluoxetine (Prozac©)
- Sertraline (Zoloft©)
- Paroxetine (Paxil©)
- Fluvoxamine (Luvox©)
- Citalopram (Celexa©)
- Escitalopram (Lexapro©)

Atypical antidepressants such as bupropion (Welbutrin©) and venlafaxine (Effexor©) are sometimes used to augment OCD medication. It is critical that people seek treatment from specialists in their area, so that medication can be properly prescribed and monitored.

## 1.22. Behavioral Interventions for OCD

A researched and tested behavioral therapy called cognitive behavioral therapy (CBT) has proven helpful for many people with OCD.

- At the core of this behavior therapy is a technique similar to exposure and response prevention based on the process of habituation.
- Many doctors and therapists who treat OCD use a combination of medication and CBT for optimum results.

   Again, it is critically important to locate doctors who specialize in treating this spectrum of disorders. Local Tourette Syndrome and OCD chapters and agencies can assist you with this search.

# Section Two

# UNDERSTANDING THE IMPACT OF TS AND OCD

2.1.  Why It Can Be Difficult to Recognize TS and OCD

2.2.  The Impact of TS and OCD on the Family

2.3.  The Impact of TS on School Performance

2.4.  The Impact of OCD on School Performance

2.5.  Tips for Accentuating the Positive

2.6.  Tips for Ensuring Success at School

## 2.1. Why It Can Be Difficult to Recognize TS and OCD

One of the most difficult concepts for parents as well as educators can be recognizing and appreciating the impact that TS and/ or OCD have on learning, performance, the family, behavior, and social and emotional well-being. Following are a number of the reasons for this:

- Both of these disorders can manifest themselves in an enormous variety of ways.

- Many people do not recognize what a tic is or when a student is obsessing about something.

- Children with TS try very hard to hide or camouflage their symptoms.

- Obsessions are "tics of the mind," so they are not always visible, and unless one knows the red flags to look for they often go unnoticed or, even worse, misunderstood by parents and educators.

- Many parents and educators have limited understanding of the associated disorders on the spectrum with TS and often view them as bad behavior.

## 2.2. The Impact of TS and OCD on the Family

Both TS and OCD can significantly affect the entire family in a variety of ways:

- Raising a child with TS and/or OCD often puts a great strain on the marital relationship, and siblings without the disorder can also be affected.

- Children with these disorders try very hard to suppress symptoms as much as possible in school, which causes the tics and obsessions to be much worse at home. Home is a safe place where they can tick without fear of being teased, imitated, or punished.

- Family members are often dealing with severe motor and vocal tics at home that the outside world never sees, which can cause considerable disruption in everyday family life.

- Children with these disorders tend to come home exhausted from ticking, trying to suppress symptoms, and struggling all day with the associated disorders.

- Homework will probably take them two to three times longer than their average peers.

- This fatigue, along with the pressure to get their work done for the next day, results in meltdowns that can last for hours and that everyone in the family has to deal with.

- They often need constant monitoring and assistance as they attempt to do their work, which takes parents away from other children and their own responsibilities.

- Many children with TS also have executive dysfunction and are very disorganized. Parents regularly have to make return trips to school in the evening to obtain materials that have been left in a locker or to clarify what the assignment was because the child has not remembered to write it down.

- Despite the fact that parents understand these factors to be a part of TS, they can become easily and understandably frustrated with the child.

- Children with OCD get stuck and cannot move on, which can increase frustration for everyone, which in turn can result in confrontations between parent and child.

- In addition to being exhausting, tics can be very painful. It is emotionally very difficult for parents to watch their child struggling with tics that are causing bodily harm.

- Public outings can potentially be very troublesome, as the manifestations of the tics may be disruptive and completely misunderstood by outsiders.

  - A child with loud vocal tics will have great difficulty going out with her family to eat in a local restaurant, attending church services, shopping at the supermarket, or going to see a movie or to any of the many public places that families frequent.

  - Siblings are often embarrassed by the symptoms of the child with TS and feel guilty for being embarrassed.

- Because TS and OCD are hereditary, it is quite common for a parent who has TS or OCD on his side of the family to feel a certain amount of guilt that he has passed this on to his own children.

- Although these disorders are not degenerative or life-threatening, their progression is very unpredictable.

- It can be overwhelming to the parents as well as the child as they often look ahead to a bleak future.

- Parents struggle to distinguish the symptoms of these disorders from just plain bad behavior.

- Parenting techniques that have worked quite well with their other children don't work at all with these kids, and parents must search for different methods of dealing with them.

- Parents may be constantly battling the school system to obtain appropriate educational services for these children.

- Schools don't always understand the complexity of TS and OCD and view these children as poorly behaved, defiant, lazy, or stubborn, thus depriving them of the tools they need to be successful.

- Frequent school meetings become critical and can take parents away from their jobs, and many employers may not understand or sympathize with this need.

## 2.3. The Impact of TS on School Performance

The impact of TS on school performance is enormous and may not be recognized by the educational personnel working with these children.

- Tics themselves can be very disruptive to the child's efforts at school. The mildest tics can be the most disruptive.

- It is commonly assumed that if a tic is not disturbing other people in the classroom, it's not disturbing the child. This is generally not the case.

- Children try very hard to camouflage or suppress their tics for fear of embarrassment so the teacher may not even see the child ticking.

- Most teachers teach classes of twenty to thirty students, thus making it virtually impossible for them to monitor one child closely enough to determine which tics she has and/or is possibly trying to hide.

- Examples of the interference of motor and vocal tics are numerous:

  - An eye-blinking tic makes it impossible for a child to read, copy things from the board, and take notes. Eye blinking disturbs no one but the child with TS and is a very easy tic to camouflage.

  - Finger tics or any tic that causes hand, arm, wrist, or shoulder movement make it very difficult for a child to write.

  - Many children with TS have gross motor movements such as upper-body thrusts or twists, which can be very intrusive as well as painful.

  - The repetitiveness of both motor and vocal tics can repeatedly break the child's focus on what they are trying to accomplish or what is being taught.

  - Children are almost always embarrassed by their tics and worried that their tics may be disturbing other students.

- They spend endless amounts of time trying to suppress their symptoms, which makes it impossible to concentrate on anything else.

- Complex motor tics—such as standing up and twirling several times a class period or having to repeatedly touch the floor or clap their hands—can be especially disruptive to the child with TS.

- Tics can be exhausting, and this exhaustion is an enormous hindrance to learning and performance in a classroom setting.

- Children with TS spend a significant amount of time worrying about the social implications of their tics. Will someone make fun of them? Will someone imitate them? Will they be punished for symptoms over which they have no control?

## 2.4. The Impact of OCD on School Performance

OCD is a disorder with a variety of manifestations, which makes the list of interferences equally long. Following are specific examples of how each of the previously described OCD manifestations can interfere with learning and performance:

*The Need for Symmetry, Perfection, and Neatness*

- The need to write and then erase words over and over slows down the writing process.
- The need for a perfectly sharpened pencil leads a child to the pencil sharpener repeatedly throughout the class.
- The need to keep items lined up perfectly on a desk or to keep a locker impeccably neat takes enormous amounts of time.
- The need to fill in bubbles perfectly on a computer-generated test or assignment can be very interfering.
- The need to copy homework over and over again until it appears perfect dramatically slows down the completion of the work and creates increased frustration.

*Repeated Counting*

- Counting the words on a page as students read or write or counting ceiling tiles or the number of chairs, desks, or other students in the room impedes concentration and slows down the work process.
- Counting is rarely seen by others, including the teacher, because it's done in the person's head. The student may simply appear spacey and inattentive, and if interrupted, he becomes very anxious until he can complete the counting.

*Checking Things*

- Double-checking to make sure the combination lock on their locker is turned to prevent others from breaking into it takes endless amounts of time, which causes students to be late for the next class.

- The need to check each assignment or test repeatedly to ensure perfection produces a great deal of anxiety and delays students' ability to finish the task at hand.

### Constant Doubt or Worrying

- Students with anxiety often look like kids who are trying to avoid certain classes or avoid school entirely.
- They may need to call home several times a day to make sure their family members are OK or sit near a classroom door.
- The anxiety takes over, and they cannot concentrate on anything that is being taught.
- Constant worrying can often lead to full-blown anxiety attacks.

### Obsessive Fears

- Obsessive, irrational fears are constantly on a child's mind, interfering significantly with paying attention.
- These fears may prevent the child from getting involved in extracurricular activities or social events.
- Some children with fears related to school may be unable to come to school at all.

### Germs and Contamination

- The obsession is a fear of contamination, and the compulsion is to wash themselves or things around them many times over and over again.
- Students may step out of class repeatedly to wash their hands.
- They become anxious when someone in the class sneezes or coughs.
- They worry about catching diseases that others in the school may have.

- They may have to take very long showers, which detract from the time they need to get homework done.

### Ritualistic Behaviors

- A child may have to add a dot at the top of the page for every word that is written, which slows down the task at hand.
- She may have to hit the desk three times for every word she writes.
- She may be unable to start her work until a certain ritual is completed.
- She may have to touch the doorway four times before she walks through it.
- Rituals take time and concentration.

### Asking Repeated Questions

- Asking the same question over and over for clarification interrupts the class.
- If the child is prevented from asking the question, he becomes very anxious that he doesn't have the correct answer.
- These interruptions annoy other students and create social issues for the affected child, who is embarrassed but cannot stop asking the questions.

### Difficulty with Transitions or Any Kind of Change

- A simple transition from one activity in the classroom to another creates great anxiety because the child may feel that the first activity has not been completed to her satisfaction.
- A sudden change in the day's schedule may send her into a tailspin.
- If an activity she had looked forward to suddenly needs to be cancelled, she can barely cope, and this often results in a meltdown.

### Obsessive Sense of Justice

- A child may feel compelled to question every item that was marked wrong on their test, which irritates the teacher and disrupts the class.
- He may have a strong need to tell the teacher when he thinks another child has cheated or done something else wrong that the teacher hasn't noticed.
- He may argue with teachers and other children over insignificant issues.
- He may be unable to accept an adult's decision on a particular topic.

### Obsessive Thoughts

- Thoughts that go through a child's head over and over again are never seen by others, but interfere greatly with her ability to concentrate on what is being taught.
- Like that first song that you hear on the radio in the morning, it plays over and over in your head all day long. Obsessive thoughts can go on for months.

## 2.5. Tips for Accentuating the Positive

One of the most important things to remember about TS and OCD is that these disorders are neurological. The tics cause the body to be out of control, and the OCD causes the mental brakes to get stuck. The days can seem very long when you are constantly trying to control the uncontrollable and this massive effort is interfering with everything you try to accomplish.

Accentuating the positive is critical to the success of children with TS and OCD at home and at school. They all have talents and strengths, but these are often lost amongst the tics, obsessions, learning difficulties, and attention problems. We must peel back the layers to identify those strengths and tap into them, as well as find creative accommodations to deal with the interferences.

- There is much more to these children than their disorder; it forms only a small part of who they are.
- Because of an innate neurological "short fuse" and the levels of frustration that children with these disorders experience every day, behavioral issues often become the primary focus in their lives.
- Children with these disorders do much better with positive reinforcements than negative consequences.
- Natural consequences, if needed, usually work best. If the child destroyed something, he should replace it. If he has been rude to someone, a verbal or written apology may be in order.

## 2.6. Tips for Ensuring Success at School

The key points for ensuring success at school fall under the categories of education, communication, and cooperation.

### *Education*

- Many educators have had little or no education about Tourette Syndrome or obsessive-compulsive disorder.

- Teachers working with children with these disorders need to understand all the disorders' possible manifestations and their effects on classroom performance, learning, and behavior. This can best be accomplished by assisting the school in locating a qualified trainer who has the background and the materials to provide such training (contact your local Tourette Syndrome Association chapter or statewide TS agency).

- Several videos are available to schools for a nominal fee that can assist in providing valuable information to all staff working with the child.

### *Communication*

- The symptoms of TS and OCD wax and wane: the form and the severity of symptoms change frequently and for a variety of reasons.

- A daily communication system should be set up between home and school that will keep staff informed of the following:
  - Tics or obsessions that have recently emerged
  - Stressful or exciting situations in the child's life that could affect the severity of symptoms
  - Medication changes that may affect the child

### *Cooperation*

- A spirit of cooperation between home and school is critical.

- If parents aren't confident that the school really understands the disorders, they will not feel safe sending their child there day after day.

- Likewise, if educators believe that parents are just making excuses for their children's behavior, they will be less inclined to listen to the parents' suggestions.

### *Blame Solves Nothing*

- Blame angers parents and makes them feel inadequate and guilty.
- Blame offends and irritates teachers and administrators.
- Blame creates obstacles to communication and can only make a bad situation worse for the child in question.
- Teachers should remember that parents know their children better than anyone else and that they see many more symptoms at home than anyone sees at school.
- Teachers sometimes need to swallow their pride a bit and admit that they always have new things to learn, no matter how long they have taught.
- Parents should remember that teachers are responsible for as many as thirty children per class. They probably want to do the best for your child, but their job may at times be as overwhelming as yours.
- Parents often have to restrain themselves, put smiles on their faces, and sometimes even bring cookies.

# Section Three

## CHECKLISTS FOR PARENTS

3.1. What Parents Can Do at Home and at School to Support Children with TS and OCD

3.2. Preventing Meltdowns Through Positive Behavioral Management and Supports

3.3. Accommodations, Tips, and Environmental Changes

3.4. Managing Homework

3.5. Suggestions for School Breaks, Rainy Weekends, and Summer Vacation

3.6. School Issues

3.7. Synopsis of an Individualized Education Plan (IEP)

3.8. Tips for Being an Effective Advocate

3.9. Sample Letter for Requesting an IEP

*Note:* The checklists in Section Three are primarily intended for parents, and the checklists in Section Four are primarily intended for educators. However, you will find some overlap in the content of these two sections. This has been done purposely so that the readers who opt to read only one section will still get a complete picture. It is the author's hope that readers will read both sections to derive the full benefit from all the information offered here.

## 3.1. What Parents Can Do at Home and at School to Support Children with TS and OCD

Parenting children with TS and OCD can be overwhelming. The symptoms of these disorders are always changing, and you never know what is around the corner. It is important to remember for your own social and emotional well-being that you are not alone.

- There are many support groups across the country for families affected by TS and OCD.
- Meeting with and learning from other families dealing with the same issues can be extremely valuable educationally and can offer invaluable emotional support for you.
- Use humor as much as possible to help defuse difficult situations.
- Understand and accept that TS and OCD are not well known or understood.
- You will have to get used to always explaining to people everywhere the reason for your child's symptoms.
- Don't assume that people will automatically understand your situation, and try not to get upset when people stare or overreact. These responses are signals that it's time to put on your "advocate hat" and educate the world about TS with a smile on your face.
- Never stop educating yourself about these disorders.
  - Attend conferences, visit reputable web sites, and read everything you can get your hands on.
  - Education is the key: you will need your child's teachers to understand the disorders, so you must do the same.
- Find someone that you can talk to about what you are dealing with.
- In the same way that adults traveling on airplanes are instructed to secure their own oxygen masks before assisting their children,

you need to take care of yourself before you can help your child in everyday life.

- If you also have these disorders, take care of yourself medically so that your own symptoms won't be as interfering.
- Try not to attend school meetings alone whenever possible.
  - Bring a relative or neighbor who also knows your child or a representative from your local TS or OCD agency or parent advocacy group.
  - Parents are emotionally involved with their own children and often need to give each other breaks in a kind of tag-team approach.
- Teach your child about his disorder at age-appropriate times.
  - The books, videos, brochures, articles, and web sites listed in List 5.11 can assist you here.
  - Your child will be growing up with the disorders, and it is vitally important to give her the knowledge she needs.

### 3.2. Preventing Meltdowns Through Positive Behavioral Management and Supports

Meltdowns and repeated anger-generated episodes (RAGE) are quite common among children with these disorders. You must first determine what is causing the meltdowns or rages, much in the same way that you would solve a puzzle. You will most likely find that these rages are related to one or more of your child's neurological disorders.

Use the Home Behavior Assessment worksheet that follows to help you unravel the mystery. It should lead you to the triggers behind the behaviors, both at home and in the environment.

*Important Things to Remember as You Start This Journey*

- Teach your child that TS and OCD are reasons, not excuses, for bad behavior or not trying.
- Always accentuate the positive strengths that your child has: your child's self-esteem is critical to her future success.
- There's a fine line between accommodating and enabling.
- Never use one of your child's strengths as a consequence for bad behavior—for example, don't take away his art supplies if art is his greatest talent or source of relaxation.

# Home Behavior Assessment

1. The specific behavior observed is:

   ____ Refusal to comply       ____ Aggressive behavior
                                      toward others

   ____ Disrespect              ____ Meltdowns or rages

2. How often does the behavior occur?

   _____

3. When does the behavior most frequently occur?

   ____ During completion       ____ During transition times
        of homework

____ In unstructured or noisy environments

____ Interacting with peers or siblings

____ After school

____ When directions are given

____ When tics are worse

____ When tired

____ When things are changed

____ In response to certain sounds, clothes, smells, lights, and so on

____ Other

4. As you reflect on your responses to questions 1, 2, and 3 here, which of the following might be possible reasons for the behaviors?

____ Interfering or painful tics

____ Difficulty transitioning

____ Anxiety

____ Poor social skills

____ Difficulty with written work

____ Difficulty processing directions given

____ Interfering OCD or getting stuck

____ Sensory overload

____ Fatigue

____ Difficulty getting started on a task

____ Becoming easily overwhelmed by homework ____

Other _____

5. What environmental changes or supports are needed to decrease the likelihood of the behavior reoccurring?

____ Writing and home-work supports

____ Homework reduction

____ Organizational supports

____ Breaking down directions

____ Transition warnings

____ Social skills education

____ Warnings for changes that may happen

____ Environmental changes

____ Reduction in amount of time in unstructured situations

____ Assistance in reducing anxiety

6. Behaviors targeted:

   a. _____

   b. _____

7. Behavioral supports:

   a. _____  d. _____

   b. _____  e. _____

   c. _____  f. _____

8. Environmental changes:

   a. _____  c. _____

   b. _____  d. _____

9. Positive rewards to be provided:

   a. _____  c. _____

   b. _____  d. _____

### *Rules to Follow When Setting Up the Behavior Plan*

- The accommodations, tips, and environmental changes shown in Lists 3.3, 3.4, and 3.5 can be very useful in helping to eradicate behaviors and meltdowns.
- Never target more than one or two behaviors at a time, and be sure to target them very specifically.
- Let the child know specifically what the behavior looks like that you are trying to change. Don't just say "good behavior"; she likely will not know what that means. Instead, say: "Hitting, punching, or kicking other people is not allowed." Provide her with alternatives that she will be rewarded for using (a punching bag, a pillow to hit, a stress ball, or going for a walk, for example).
- Remember that positive rewards work much better for these kids than negative consequences.
  - Rewards don't have to be monetary; be creative.

- • The child can pick from a reward jar; earn coupons in increments of fifteen to thirty minutes of extra TV, computer, or video game time; or have a friend over. If he doesn't care about the reward, he won't work for it.
- • You know your child best and know what they will work for. Let them be a part of the process of choosing the reward.
- • Many kids need daily if not more frequent rewards. They can't wait until the weekend to see success.
- • *Be persistent*: change doesn't happen overnight. You may have to tolerate a meltdown or two before you start seeing the results you want to see.

## 3.3. Accommodations, Tips, and Environmental Changes

Teach your child coping strategies for dealing with people who stare, ask questions, and bully him. He needs to be taught what words to use to explain his symptoms as he grows and matures. This approach will help prevent meltdowns over the reactions of the people your child encounters in the environment.

- Try not to comment on or call attention to your child's symptoms as often as possible. Stress increases tics, so teaching your child to use relaxation techniques can be very helpful when tics are exacerbated.
- Many children with TS and/or OCD have accompanying sleep disorders.
  - Sleep issues may need to be dealt with medically.
  - Physicians can also make helpful suggestions for good bedtime routines. A tired child is usually a cranky child.
- Children with OCD often have a great deal of difficulty with transitions and day-to-day changes. It is crucial that parents learn the "language" they need to use with their children to help avoid meltdowns.
  - Avoid using the words "yes" or "no"; try "maybe" or "we'll see" instead.
  - Always give transition warnings in advance, such as "Dinner will be in ten minutes," rather than "Come to the table right now."
  - Instead of telling your child what's for dinner, simply say you're not sure, to avoid disappointment in case you have to change the menu.
  - Have her choose the clothes she'll be wearing tomorrow and have them laid out and ready the night before.

- Distraction can be very helpful in getting kids "unstuck" from an obsession. When kids are stuck, they often rage.
  - Get them quickly involved in something they really enjoy.
  - Use humor. Use humor. Use humor.
- Parents can help their children learn and use their own strategies for coping with symptoms, whether they are tics or obsessions.
  - Help them imagine that they carry with them a toolbox of strategies that they can use whenever they become overwhelmed.
  - Parents need to give children these strategies, teach them to rely on the strategies, and, most important, reward them when they use the strategies successfully and avoid meltdowns.
- Many children with TS have sensory issues and will often be overwhelmed by all the sensory input in their environment.
  - Children may not be able to wear certain clothes, eat certain foods, or tolerate certain sounds or bright lights.
  - If you force a child to wear a shirt with a tag or socks with seams, for example, her day will be miserable and she will be much more likely to melt down or have some behavioral issue.
  - When children with TS and OCD are in noisy environments, they are much more likely to become out of sorts.
  - There may be certain sounds that they cannot tolerate at all—such as someone chewing or a lawn mower. These sounds are like nails on a chalkboard to them.
  - Work with an occupational therapist who can teach the family strategies and therapies to help kids manage their environment. (Insurance often covers outside occupational therapy, and parents can learn to continue the therapies at home.)
- *Don't sweat the small stuff!* Pick your battles.
  - Look for shirts that have no labels (available from retailers like Soft; www.softclothing.net), or cut out the labels yourself.

- When you shop at brick-and-mortar stores, have your child try on clothes before you buy to be sure they "feel right" to them.
- Putting children's clothes in the dryer just before they put them on makes the clothes feel softer and more comfortable.
- If children want to wear the same types of clothes every day, let them.
- If your child tells you that, for example, he can't stand to hear his father chew, believe him. Let him wear a headset during dinner or eat in a separate room.
- Avoid loud, chaotic environments as much as possible. Teach your child the words to use in such situations to let you know that she can't tolerate these surroundings so that you can help her remove herself.

- When your child comes home from school, he will most likely need some wind-down time before starting homework. He has a movement disorder, and he needs to move.
  - Any type of exercise program can be very useful.
  - The exercise can be riding her bike around the neighborhood, swimming, or walking (or running) the dog.
  - Exercise changes brain chemistry and helps release the stored-up energy from the long school day.
- Make sure that your child gets enough sleep.
  - Fatigue not only makes these children cranky but also increases the severity of symptoms.
  - A bedtime routine at the same time each night will help.
  - Children may need extra wind-down time about a half hour or so before bedtime.
  - Tics can be very interfering when children are trying to get to sleep, so if they are more relaxed before they go to bed, they will fall asleep faster.
- Never give children more than one chore or direction at a time.

- If you give them three things to do, they will most likely only process one of those three things and completely ignore the other two.

- Give them one job or direction, and ask them to come back and check with you. Then give them the second one.

- Put a checklist on the refrigerator that they can check off as they accomplish the chores.

- Use visuals. They can often process visuals much better than the spoken or written word. (Display pictures of all the things in their morning routine in the order they need to do them, for example.)

# 3.4. Managing Homework

Set up a quiet place for children to do their homework at the same time each night. Most children with these disorders will need some assistance with their homework.

- They may have a great deal of trouble getting started on an assignment.
- They may need directions to be clarified.
- Break down the assignment into more manageable parts: children with these disorders become quickly overwhelmed.
  - Section off the math problems.
  - Give the child one sheet at a time and then fold it in half horizontally. Ask her to complete each part before checking with you and going on to the next.
  - Write each assignment on an index card. Let the child pick one to start with at random and put the other cards away until the first assignment is done; then rip up the card.
  - It's often a good idea to start with the most difficult assignment first, when your child is fresher.
- Scheduling frequent breaks while children do homework can be very important.
- Continued praise as they accomplish each task goes a long way toward helping them stick with it.
- Many children with these disorders benefit greatly from doing their homework on a computer because of interfering tics, obsessions, and dysgraphia. Computers also help them focus better. Young children may even need you to scribe for them.
- Wearing a headset that plays white noise or music while doing independent work can help tremendously by blocking out extraneous distracting noises that others may not notice.
- Allowing your child to chew gum or have a crunchy snack while he works also helps concentration.

- Be sure that your child's 504 Accommodation Plan (see List 5.3) or individualized education plan (IEP; see Lists 3.7 and 3.9) includes accommodations for organization.
  - Teachers need to verify and initial the homework assignment to make sure it is written down correctly in the student's notebook.
  - Ensure that someone at school is assigned to assist the child with packing up his backpack at the end of the day to make sure he has everything he needs to take home with him.
  - Study guides are essential for these children and can be written into the 504 Accommodation Plan or IEP as an accommodation.
- Become familiar with your school's homework web site.
  - The web sites of almost all schools include a page where individual teachers can record their assignments each day: that will become your favorite web page.
  - Many schools are using programs like Blackboard, where teachers can input class notes, study guides, and project and assignment guidelines.
- Request an extra set of textbooks to be kept at home.
- When tics are particularly problematic, you may need to assist your child even more than usual—for example, you may need to read for her and write for her.
- Look for a high school or college student who can, for a nominal fee, become a homework buddy for your child for a few nights a week or on the weekend.
  - The parent is always emotionally involved, so having someone else to step in can give everyone a much-needed break.
- It may be a good idea to add homework reduction to your child's 504 Accommodation Plan or IEP.
  - Suggest that the school give the parents the right to "sign off" on an incomplete assignment when the child is having an exacerbated tic episode and simply cannot finish the work.

- You can ask for extended time on homework assignments, just as you do for tests. Sometimes a one-day grace period can make a huge difference.

- Give your child choices, such as: "You can write your homework, do it on the computer, or I can scribe for you. Which do you prefer?"

- He will soon realize that he has options, which can make the work easier for him.

## 3.5. Suggestions for School Breaks, Rainy Weekends, and Summer Vacation

Summer vacation and school breaks are great times for kids to escape the pressures of school, get outdoors, run around, and use up all that energy, just to have fun. There is nothing more important for kids with TS and OCD than getting away from the stress and anxiety that school brings. These are also great times to accomplish things that cannot be done while school is in session.

Vacations and breaks are also good times to pursue activities that can be critically important to your child's success in the educational arena. Following is a list of suggestions for vacation or weekend "projects" that can be fun as well as improve your child's skills in several areas:

- If your child is going into middle school, where she will have a personal locker for the first time, go out early in the summer and buy that dreaded combination lock that will most likely give her no end of difficulty. She can practice with it each day during the summer months until she has the combination and the technique down pat. This will be one less source of stress once school begins.

Many students with TS and associated disorders have tremendous difficulty with anything that requires handwriting. The most efficient and least stressful way to complete schoolwork for these children is on a computer. Many schools, however, no longer teach keyboarding, which is a critical skill for these kids.

- Suggest that your child get involved in a vacation project that involves using the computer, such as:
  - Writing a neighborhood newspaper
  - Making labels for items around the house
  - Typing up sports stats or whatever else they may be interested in as a way to practice

- Go to the local library or computer store and find a learn-to-type program that your child can practice with a few times a week, such as:
  - Super Mario Learns to Type
  - Mavis Beacon Learn to Type
  - Disney's Adventures in Typing with Timon and Pumba (ages six and up), Read, Write & Type (ages six through eight)
  - JumpStart Typing (ages seven through ten)
  - Slam Dunk Typing (ages ten and up; targets basketball- and video-game-loving teenagers)
- To help with organizational tasks that school will require, purchase the necessary folders in a variety of colors for the fall.
  - Make labels for all of the folders (another way to practice typing with fun fonts), decorate them with your child's favorite pictures, and fill each folder with notebook paper.
  - You can do one folder at a time and spread out the fun (we hope!).
  - When school starts, you can create a cover for each textbook that matches the folder for that subject.
  - A Trapper Keeper type of binder, where all folders can be kept together and zipped in, may work best and prevent a great many losses.
  - You can also put a three-hole pencil and supply bag in the Trapper Keeper so that pens, pencils, erasers, ruler, and such are easier to keep track of.
  - Establish a separate homework folder where completed homework for each subject will be placed to keep better track of it.
- If these preparations can be made over the summer and the child can help, he will be more excited about the new system and actually take ownership of what he has created.
- Many kids with TS find it difficult to sit still and read because of interfering tics or hyperactivity.

- Many of the classic books that kids will need to read in school are available as books on CD, iPod, or other media, at the library.
- If you can find out which books will be assigned next year, this is a great way to get kids used to books on tape and to get a head start on next year.

## 3.6. School Issues

- Arrange a peer in-service at your child's school. This program can be set up by someone from the local TS or OCD agency or by school personnel. (The peer in-service model shown in List 4.5 can be used by school personnel.)

- The Tourette Syndrome Association offers videos that schools can use for peer in-service programs.

- Make sure that your child's 504 Accommodation Plan or individualized education plan (IEP) includes a provision that every teacher and staff member who comes into contact with your child receives training at the beginning of each school year about these disorders.

  - Some schools will say that this cannot be done because of teacher contracts or other barriers.

  - Suggest that it be done during a monthly mandatory staff meeting, at a staff development day, or during teacher planning time, so as not to infringe on the teachers' contract.

- Set up a communication plan with your child's teachers so that you can monitor how things at school are going on a regular basis.

  - The communication plan enables you to inform teachers and staff about ever-changing symptoms.

  - E-mail and the student's agenda book are good tools for these communications.

- Be sure to read Lists 4.7, 4.9, and 4.14 to learn what you can request of the school and what may help at home in this regard.

- We often assume that all teachers read the IEP or 504 Accommodation Plan from cover to cover, but this is not always a reality.

- Prepare a single- or double-sided sheet to introduce your child to all the teachers who will be working with her that school year. This IEP synopsis should focus first on strengths, followed by areas of weakness, and go on to discuss the accommodations that all teachers are responsible for from the 504 Accommodation Plan or IEP. List 3.7 shows a sample of such a document.

## 3.7. Synopsis of an Individualized Education Plan (IEP)

# Synopsis of IEP for John Q. Tourette

*Classification:* Other Health Impaired

*Diagnosis:* Tourette Syndrome, ADHD, obsessive-compulsive disorder, anxiety disorder, sensory integration difficulties, dysgraphia

*Services:* Occupational therapy, shared aide, consultant teacher services, counseling

*Strengths:* Very bright, excellent reader, eager to learn and do well in school, very interested in science and public speaking

## Problem Areas

- Math
- Handwriting and other fine motor activities
- Short attention span
- Sensory overload in noisy, chaotic environments
- Interfering tics associated with Tourette Syndrome
- Organization
- Gross motor deficits
- Difficulty with motor planning; fine and gross motor activities
- Interfering obsessions and compulsions

## Accommodations

- Frequent breaks from class to release tics
- Daily journal or communication log between home and school

- Assignments verified by teacher

- Long-range assignments broken down into smaller parts

- Reduction in length of homework assignments

- Instructions repeated and reread for clarification

- Preferential seating at front and near the side of classroom

- Reminders to help refocus when inattentive

- Extended time for tests and testing in a quiet location

- Alternatives to long written assignments (scribe, computer, or other similar assignments)

- At the end of each day teacher or aide will ensure that needed materials are in the student's backpack to take home

- Assistance with noisy unstructured environments such as PE, hallways, or cafeteria

- Positive Behavior Intervention Plan

## Things to Avoid

- Seating too close to other children because of tics and sensory issues

- Being in the middle of a line: John is much better at the beginning or the end

## 3.8. Tips for Being an Effective Advocate

As the one who knows your child the best, you are her best advocate. You must educate yourself about all the services that are available for your child and what she is entitled to. (See Lists 5.1 through 5.6 for further information on the educational rights of children with TS and OCD.) Your ability to help your child is vastly improved when you know what she is entitled to. The resources given in List 5.11 will help you become a more effective advocate.

- Check with your local Parent Training and Information Center (PTI; www.taalliance.org), a federal agency with offices in every state. Not only will they often provide you with an advocate, but they will also offer workshops for parents on how to understand and access the special education system.

- Contact your local Tourette Syndrome Association or OCD chapter or state agency to locate someone who can assist you and attend school meetings with you.

- Once you have decided that your child is in need of services at school, you will need to write a letter requesting these services.

  - This letter should be sent to the director of special education for the school district that your child attends and/or your child's building principal.

  - The letter should be accompanied by a letter from the treating physician stating all the diagnoses your child has.

  - List 3.9 shows a sample letter that you can adapt for this purpose. Once this letter is received, the school has a certain time frame in which to complete the requested evaluations and meet to discuss classification and services. This time frame varies by state.

- Always try to bring an advocate along to school meetings regarding 504 Plans or IEPs, poor grades, or behavioral issues. Emotions can get the better of you in such meetings, and you may very well need someone to carry on if the tears start.

- Again, contact your local Tourette Syndrome or OCD chapter or agency, ask another parent who may have experience with the special education process, or find an advocate through your local PTI.

- Keep all of your paperwork organized. (PTIs often offer workshops on Keeping a Binder for your child.)

- Be assertive, but not aggressive. It is always in the best interest of your child that you "keep your cool."

  - Take a break from the meeting when you need to. If things are heating up, ask that the meeting be tabled and resumed at a later date.

  - Letters from treating physicians or counselors can be very helpful—then your points are reinforced and documented by the authority of medical professionals. (See List 5.5 for a sample physician's letter.)

- An educated advocate is an effective advocate.

  - Educate yourself about TS and associated disorders and their effects on learning, performance, and social and emotional well-being.

  - Don't be upset when school personnel don't have a great knowledge base on TS; this disorder is still not a significant part of a college curriculum in most colleges and universities.

  - Do bring brochures or videos to school to help educate the teachers, but *don't* overwhelm them. They simply do not have the time to read everything that parents suggest, so pick and choose such resources wisely.

## 3.9. Sample Letter for Requesting an IEP

---

### Sample School Letter

Dear _____,

    My child, _____, has recently been diagnosed with Tourette Syndrome by Dr. _____. Tourette Syndrome is a neurological spectrum disorder, which is almost always accompanied by other neurological disorders. He/She has also been diagnosed with attention deficit hyperactivity disorder (ADHD) and obsessive compulsive disorder (OCD). I have observed the impact that all of these disorders are having on his/her academic performance and social and emotional well-being. I have also learned from TS literature that a very large number of children with TS also experience learning disabilities. These disabilities very often include auditory processing difficulties, fine motor impairment, visual motor impairment, and executive dysfunction.

    I am therefore requesting that my child be observed and tested by the school psychologist as the first step in seeking from the Special Education Committee a classification of Other Health Impaired. Given the high percentage of children with TS who do have these accompanying disorders, I am also requesting both an occupational therapy evaluation and a speech evaluation.

    I am including a letter of diagnosis from the treating physician, which also discusses the urgent need for the completion of all of the above requested evaluations. In the interim, I will be more than happy to meet with school personnel working with my child to discuss what behaviors he/she may be exhibiting in the classroom as a result of this diagnosis and what educators can do to assist.

    Thank you for your prompt attention to this matter. I look forward to hearing from you soon and to working together with school personnel to provide an optimum learning environment for my child.

    Sincerely,

---

# Section Four

## CHECKLISTS FOR TEACHERS

4.1. Top Ten Things Teachers Need to Know About Students with Tourette Syndrome

4.2. Tips for Working with Students with TS and OCD in the Classroom

4.3. Tips for Training Staff on Working with Students with TS and OCD

4.4. Tips for Educating Peers About TS and OCD

4.5. A Peer In-Service Model

4.6. Strategies for Dealing with Motor and Vocal Tics in the Classroom

4.7. Accommodating Motor Tics

4.8. Dealing with Vocal Tics

4.9. Accommodating Vocal Tics

4.10. Attitude Is Everything

4.11. Classroom Observation Form

4.12. Tips for Addressing Challenging Behaviors

4.13. Functional Behavioral Assessment and Positive Behavior Intervention Plan for Students with TS, OCD, and ADHD

4.14. Accommodations for Associated Disorders

## 4.1. Top Ten Things Teachers Need to Know About Tourette Syndrome

1. Tourette Syndrome is a medical disorder caused by a chemical imbalance in the brain. To have a diagnosis of TS, you must have multiple motor tics, at least one vocal tic, waxing and waning of symptoms, symptoms that last at least a year, and childhood onset of symptoms between the ages of two and eighteen.

2. You may believe you know all there is to know about TS, but you probably know only one-tenth of what you actually need to know. The key to demystifying TS and solving the majority of classroom problems is accurate information.

3. The only consistent thing about TS is inconsistency. No two children with TS are alike, and no child with TS will exhibit the same symptoms and have the same difficulties every day.

4. The worst things an educator can do are to ask a child to stop ticking and to constantly question which movements or vocalizations are tics and which are not.

5. TS is almost always accompanied by other neurological disorders.

6. A major component of TS is a symptom known as *dysinhibition*, or difficulty in consistently inhibiting thoughts and/or actions. Inappropriate statements or behaviors very frequently result from the student's inability to consistently apply "mental brakes."

7. Working with students with TS and any of its associated disorders can be very challenging. Your most important and valuable attribute will become your creativity and your ability to think "outside the box."

8. Listen to the child's parents. They know their child better than anyone else and can be an invaluable resource. Don't assume that they are just making excuses for their child.

9. Children with neurological disorders respond much better to positive, proactive interventions than negative consequences.

10. The information offered in this book will expand your knowledge of TS and give you the practical tools you need to effectively deal with TS in your classroom.

## 4.2. Tips for Working with Students with TS and OCD in the Classroom

TS and OCD are very complex disorders that are ever changing and can vary significantly from individual to individual. Symptoms not only vary from individual to individual but also can change at a moment's notice in one child.

- Remember that one of the diagnostic criteria for a diagnosis of TS is waxing and waning of symptoms.

- Comorbid disorders also vary tremendously from person to person and can change the whole profile of the child.

- Tics and obsessions can be very complex and often look like behaviors.

- Frequent communication between home and school is critical to stay informed of these constantly changing symptoms.

- Medications can cause side effects, which also may be misinterpreted. Parents should keep their child's educators informed of medication changes, and educators should likewise inform parents about sudden changes they see in the child at school.

- Keeping the school nurse involved is an excellent idea.

- Avail yourself of brochures and videos that will help you better understand what TS and OCD really look like.

- *Listen* to what parents are telling you; they know their child.

- Parents almost always report that symptoms are worse at home, which is definitely true.

- Children try very hard to suppress symptoms at school, but the symptoms eventually will come out.

- The amount of homework assigned may need to be reduced. It can take these children twice as long to complete their assignments because of the interference of tics, obsessions, distractibility, and dysgraphia.
  - These children may need extra time for long assignments and projects.

- Parents may need to be given permission to sign off on homework when the child simply cannot do any more.
- Providing an appropriate environment in the classroom takes planning, creativity, and persistence, as well as effective and appropriate strategies to accommodate the needs of the student with TS along with the rest of the class.

## 4.3. Tips for Training Staff on Working with Students with TS and OCD

There are many effective ways of training staff; see the numerous excellent brochures and videos listed in List 5.11. Contact your local Tourette Syndrome Association (TSA) or OCD chapter or state TS agency and ask someone from that agency to do a staff training. They frequently have trainers available who can include appropriate strategies and accommodations as a part of the training.

Several states do not have active chapters or agencies, and in these cases I recommend an educator's in-service DVD titled A *Teacher Looks at Tourette Syndrome*. This is a video of me presenting a workshop to educators and is available through TSA (www.tsa-usa.org).

Training of *all* staff working with this child is crucial. Remember to include the following:

- Special area teachers (art, music, technology, and so on)
- The school bus driver
- The librarian
- The cafeteria monitor
- Any others who come into contact with the child at school

## 4.4. Tips for Educating Peers About TS and OCD

Many issues that children with TS and OCD face are social or emotional in nature and result from ignorance on the part of their peers as to why they are exhibiting often bizarre symptoms.

- Children will tease, make fun of, and even fear what they don't understand.
- Once peers are educated in an appropriate manner, the vast majority of these social and emotional problems disappear.
- Because of privacy issues, it is mandatory that the school obtains the permission of the parents before such a presentation is done.
- If a child or the parents are opposed to educating their peers, this training may be given instead through a generic presentation to a science class, a health class, or as part of a disabilities awareness program, which many schools offer already.
- If you organize a peer in-service program for students in your class or school, be sure to include parents of other students in the class as well.
- Because of a lack of understanding, many times children have spoken to their parents about a classmate who makes noises in class or says inappropriate things.
  - Other parents may also have concerns about this child.
  - Send out a letter informing the other parents of such a presentation. The sample letter that follows can be used for this purpose.

Dear Parents,

We wanted to let parents know that we have a student in our class this year who has Tourette Syndrome (TS). TS is a neurological disorder characterized by involuntary movements and vocalizations referred to as motor and vocal tics. Tourette Syndrome is much more common than we once thought, and we have several students in the district diagnosed with this disorder. This is a hereditary disorder, and it is certainly not contagious. Students with TS usually have average to above-average intelligence and go on to be doctors, lawyers, teachers, and any other type of professional they choose to be. The vocal tics can be loud at times, but because we have had class discussions about this, the children have been very understanding and this delightful young child is completely accepted by all the students.

In the near future we will be asking someone from a local Tourette Syndrome agency to come in and speak to the class about this syndrome, and we will also be inviting parents to attend if they are able.

We see this as a wonderful opportunity to teach our students about differences and acceptance and, in particular, about TS. We also thank this child's parents for giving us the permission to provide this learning experience for the other children in the school.

## 4.5. A Peer In-Service Model

You may be able to find someone through your local Tourette Syndrome agency who is trained to do a peer in-service. If not, following is a peer in-service model that the school psychologist, social worker, counselor, school nurse, special education, or regular education teacher can present to the class or the team. It is a program about differences that leads to a discussion about TS and OCD and can be adjusted to any age level. It can be done by itself or used in combination with a peer in-service DVD entitled *I Have Tourette's But Tourette's Doesn't Have Me*. This DVD was produced by the HBO network in conjunction with the Tourette Syndrome Association (TSA) and won an Emmy in 2008 for best children's documentary. It is available through HBO or TSA (www.tsa-usa.org).

---

### Educating Classmates About Tourette Syndrome

#### Five Steps to Successful Peer Training: A Program About Differences

1. *Do not begin your in-service by talking immediately about TS.* Talk first about other traits and medical conditions that the students might already know about. You may begin your in-service by asking questions such as:

- Raise your hand if you have blond hair (or brown hair or black hair or red hair).

- Raise your hand if you have curly hair (or straight hair or brown eyes or blue eyes).

- Raise your hand if you have freckles.

- Where do all these varied traits come from? (Seek a response from parents here.)

- What are these inherited traits called? (Heredity or genetics.)

*(continued)*

(continued)

- How many of you have ever been told that you look like one of your parents?

- What good traits have you inherited from your parents? (Artistic ability, musical ability, athletic talent, or nice hair, for example.)

- Has anyone inherited something from their parents that they don't like? (Big feet, freckles, curly hair, too tall, too short, for example.)

- What can you do about these things? (Not much.) For example, can you erase your freckles?

- Has anyone ever been made fun of for something they can't help?

- How did that make you feel?

## Medical Issues

- Does anyone know anything about asthma? Tell me what you know.

- What part of your body does asthma affect?

- Does anyone have asthma themselves or know someone with asthma?

- Have you ever seen anyone use an inhaler for an asthma attack?

- Would you think of making fun of someone that you saw using an inhaler?

- What about diabetes?

   [Continue with questions similar to those posed about asthma.]

- What would be bad about having asthma or diabetes?

2. *Now is the time to introduce Tourette Syndrome.* If you have the disorder, you can ask students if they have noticed things that you have been doing that seem a little different. If you don't have TS, you could begin by asking whether anyone knows of any disorders that affect the brain. One example is someone who has had a head injury from an accident and can no longer walk or someone who has cerebral palsy. You can ask questions such as:

- What does your brain control? (Speech and movement, for example.)
- Does anyone know a brain disorder that affects movement?

This discussion will help lead the group to TS. The following explanation of TS may help:

With TS it's like your brain is lacking stop signs. The average person moves only when they want to move. When you have TS, your body moves when you don't want it to. We call these movements "tics." Take time to present the following explanation of a tic:

- A tic is a rapid repetitive movement of any muscular group in your body.
- A tic can be a shoulder shrug, an eye blink, a facial twitch, an arm or leg jerk, a finger tapping, or a more complex movement like hopping, twirling, jumping, or clapping.
- Try to use examples of tics that the child in question may have.

Talk about vocal tics.

- A tic can also be a noise that a person makes or a word that he says over and over again.
- A vocal tic can include sniffing, throat clearing, a squeak, a grunt, or simply a word or phrase that is repeated.

*(continued)*

*(continued)*

3. *The next area to explore is the cause of TS.*

- We don't really know the cause, but we do know that TS is hereditary.

- Remember all the hereditary traits we talked about that we get from our parents.

  - Hair color

  - Eye color

  - Freckles

  - Certain abilities

Is it nice to make fun of things people have no control over? Everybody has something about himself or herself that they are sensitive about. Some people with freckles hate their freckles.

4. *The next area to discuss is the fact that TS is not contagious and no one ever dies from it.* You might then ask the following question:

- If it's not contagious and you won't die from it, what is so bad about having TS? Try to elicit the following three responses:

  - People make fun of you and imitate you because they don't understand your situation.

  - Tics can interfere with what you're trying to accomplish. For example, if you had a tic that involved constantly blinking your eyes, it would be hard to read, copy things from the blackboard, or watch TV. If you had a finger or hand tic, it would be hard to write.

  - Tics hurt. Your body is not supposed to constantly move like that. Head jerking tics cause neck pain. Eye-blinking tics can cause eyestrain and headaches.

5. *If the child in question has obvious signs of OCD and/or ADHD, you might also explore these two disorders.* Stick with symptoms that are obvious. This is a good opportunity to ask the following questions:

- Has anyone ever had a sneeze that they were trying to hold in? That's what a tic feels like. You try and try to suppress it, but eventually it has to come out.

- Does anyone follow baseball or soccer? Does anyone know the name of a professional baseball player who has TS? This is a perfect time to talk about Jim Eisenreich, a former professional baseball player who has TS. Eisenreich played for several baseball teams, including the Marlins, the Phillies, the Royals, and the Twins. His baseball career almost came to a sudden end when he was twenty-eight years old and was still undiagnosed with TS.

- Tim Howard, the professional soccer player who was goalie for Team USA in the 2010 World Cup series, has TS and OCD.

- Howie Mandell, host of *Deal or No Deal,* has OCD. He has written a book about it called *Here's the Deal: Don't Touch Me.*

- Samuel Johnson, who wrote the first English dictionary, had TS.

Anyone can get TS, just as anyone can have asthma or diabetes. It doesn't change who we are. We are all different, and that's what makes us special. We should celebrate differences. The world would be a very boring place if we all looked and acted the same.

## 4.6. Strategies for Dealing with Motor and Vocal Tics in the Classroom

Students with TS and OCD may exhibit symptoms unlike any other disorder you've ever dealt with in your classroom. Your accommodations might have to be "outside the box," unlike any other solutions or strategies you've used before.

Speak frankly with and listen openly to the parents, the child, and the treating physician before determining which areas are problematic for the child in question. A teacher may not be able to observe every symptom a child is exhibiting. This is because children with TS:

- Often try to suppress or camouflage tics that they feel might be disturbing to the class or might call unwanted and embarrassing attention to themselves.
- Rarely share their hidden OCD symptoms with a teacher. You will need to look for "red flags."

When you've explored the situation by talking openly, listening acutely, and reading thoroughly, you will have a better handle on what is interfering with the child's ability to be academically successful.

## 4.7. Accommodating Motor Tics

- Tests should be administered in a separate location with time limits waived or extended.

- Educate the other students who come into contact with the child with TS. (See the peer in-service model in List 4.5 in this section.)

- Provide a refuge where the student can go to calm down and release tics or obsessions, such as the nurse's office or the school psychologist's office. The principal's office should be avoided, as this may be perceived as a punishment.

- Give frequent breaks outside the classroom to release tics in a less embarrassing environment such as:
  - The bathroom
  - The drinking fountain
  - A real or invented errand to run
  - A laminated pass for a quick exit from class when a short break is needed

- Provide a safe place in the school for the child to go for a few minutes as needed.

- Give the child a set of seven or eight passes to use for the day.
  - Each pass can represent a three- to four-minute break outside the classroom.
  - Be specific as to where the child can go and how many passes she can use per class period or block of time; this encourages students to learn to self-monitor.

- Seat the student with TS in an area where his tics will be less noticeable and embarrassing.

- Never seat him in the center front of the classroom.

- Assess the interference of individual tics.
  - Tics such as eye blinking, eye scrunching, or head shaking may necessitate assistance with reading and/or writing.

- Hand or finger tics may require assistance with writing.
- Environmental accommodations may be necessary for children with inappropriate touching tics. (See the Appendix for anecdotal examples of these tics.)
- If tics are socially inappropriate (such as spitting, swearing, licking things, or touching people inappropriately), it may be necessary to brainstorm possible solutions.
  - A spitting tic can often be resolved by giving the child a tissue to spit into, gum to chew, or hard candy or a lollipop to suck on.
- Try scheduling core academics at or near the beginning of the day, because tics tend to worsen when a child is tired.
- Communicate with parents frequently, and report worsening tics or the development of new ones.
- Create a supportive, accepting classroom environment. Students will feel safer, and this will alleviate much of the anxiety and frustration, which will help reduce tics.
- The teacher is always the role model. Set a tone that is accepting and tolerant of the child's symptoms, and this will naturally dictate how the other students treat that child.

## 4.8. Dealing with Vocal Tics

Remember the old adage "Beauty is in the eye of the beholder"? In the same vein, "Vocal tics are only disruptions in the eye of the beholder." It is first and foremost your understanding of and second your attitude toward the vocal tics that will make or break your success at having a child in your class with TS. Remember:

- Tics are involuntary.

- TS is highly suggestible: the more a student is told not to do the vocal or motor tics, the more they have to do them.

- When a person with TS knows that vocal tics are unacceptable in a certain setting, the tics are more likely to occur in that setting.

- Tics almost always worsen with stress, anxiety, excitement, and fatigue.

- Coprolalia (involuntary uttering of inappropriate words or phrases) may occur at random, but it can also appear to fit the situation perfectly. A child may need to use an ethnic slur only when he sees someone of that ethnicity.

## 4.9. Accommodating Vocal Tics

- The most effective plan is simply ignoring the tics, and this approach can be role-modeled by the teacher.

- The second most effective strategy is to educate everyone, including the other students in the class. (See the peer in-service model in List 4.5.)

- Give the child frequent breaks outside the classroom to release tics in a more private, less embarrassing environment.

  - It is not a good idea to suggest to the child that she needs to leave the room because that in itself can be stressful.

  - Errands are great ways to give kids breaks without causing them to feel they're not wanted in the classroom.

- In the case of very loud, disruptive vocal tics, set up a private place in the school where a computer with a video cam can be set up with access to Skype (www.skype.com), a software application that allows users to make free voice calls and video conference using the Internet.

  - The teacher can also have a similar setup in the classroom.

  - When the child feels that vocal tics are becoming very disruptive, they can go to their special location, turn on Skype, and still be able to listen to what is being taught.

- Hanging a sign in the main office can help alleviate visitors' concerns about coprolalia. A sample sign can be found on page 150 in the Appendix.

## 4.10. Attitude Is Everything

Vocal tics only appear to be disruptive because they are different from what we are used to experiencing in a classroom.

- Use the classroom observation form in List 4.11 as follows:
  - In one column is a list of interruptions that occur in classrooms across the country every day.
  - In the other column you can track the vocal tics of the student with TS.
- In 100 percent of the many observations I have done, normal classroom interruptions far outnumber the noise from vocal tics of students with TS.
- Once everyone understands the disorder, they become as accustomed to hearing vocal tics as they are to hearing the other usual noises in the classroom.
- The teacher is the role model in the classroom who can escalate or deescalate a situation simply through his reaction to it.
- A teacher can allow a child to thrive and be accepted and should role-model for the other students that being different is to be tolerated and even encouraged.

## 4.11. Classroom Observation Form

### Classroom Interruptions – Vocal Tics (Keep Count)

Vocal tics _____

Coughing _____

Sneezing _____

Blowing nose _____

Sharpening pencil _____

Intercom _____

Student shouting out _____

Phone ringing _____

Someone dropping something _____

Pencil tapping _____

Foot tapping or shuffling _____

Someone at classroom door _____

Other (list) _____

## 4.12. Tips for Addressing Challenging Behaviors

Neurological disorders can be very complex. With accurate knowledge about TS and related disorders, however, behavioral assessments of students with these disorders do not have to be frightening and overwhelming. The team conducting such an assessment should include someone who is very knowledgeable about TS and its associated disorders or is willing to educate themselves.

Some children with these disorders are predisposed to low frustration tolerance. However:

- The behaviors they exhibit are almost always triggered by one or more of their neurological disorders.
- It is up to the professional to determine what is causing the behavior or meltdown and put into place appropriate strategies, environmental accommodations, and positive interventions to help prevent the recurrence of these behaviors.

See the Functional Behavioral Assessment (FBA) and the Positive Behavior Intervention Plan (PBIP) in List 4.13, which have been created for children with TS, OCD, ADHD, and other neurological disorders. Be sure to read the accompanying guidelines before using these assessments.

## 4.13. Functional Behavioral Assessment and Positive Behavior Intervention Plan for Students with TS, OCD, and ADHD

The Individuals with Disabilities Education Act (IDEA) 2004 requires that a Functional Behavior Assessment (FBA) be conducted and a positive behavior intervention plan be developed whenever the behavior of a student interferes with the ability of that student or other students to learn. (See Lists 5.2, 5.3, 5.4, 5.5, and 5.6 for an in-depth discussion of IDEA.)

- Conducting an FBA for a classified child with a disability exhibiting "behavior problems" is no longer an option; it is the law.
- An FBA is the *process* of determining why an individual engages in challenging behaviors and how the behavior relates to the environment.
- Conducting an FBA for a child with TS can be very challenging. TS is one of the most complex and commonly misunderstood neurological disorders that educators are likely to encounter.
- Erroneous assumptions are often made about the reason for the behaviors of these children.
- Behavior plans should *never* address tics.
  - However, if the tic is self-injurious or socially *very* inappropriate, environmental changes and supports may be necessary. (See the anecdotal examples given in the Appendix)
- In a middle or high school setting, be sure that *at least* four to six teachers or support personnel who work closely with the student complete the worksheet portion of the assessment.
- In an elementary school setting, the classroom teacher and *at least* two to five other special teachers or support personnel should complete the worksheet.
- A key member of the child's educational team should then compile the results of the worksheets onto the actual FBA

summary form. Be sure to use the facts and conclusions on the FBA to create the positive behavior intervention plan (PBIP).

- Read through the anecdotal materials in the Appendix of this book before beginning to complete the worksheets.

- Observe the student in the environments where the behavior in question is most likely to occur.

  - This may be in nonclassroom settings such as the cafeteria or hallways.

  - Look at specific tasks, various elements of the task, instructional style, the reaction of other students, and TS or OCD symptoms to determine how the environment affects the behavior.

- The ultimate purpose of this assessment is to limit the likelihood of the behaviors recurring by providing accommodations, changing the environment or teaching skills, and/or suggesting replacement behaviors.

- Make sure that the child's parents are involved whenever possible.

- Always ask yourself *what you can do* **for** *the child using positive behavior interventions to prevent the behavior, instead of looking at what to do* **to** *the child after the behavior occurs.*

- In my experience having facilitated hundreds of FBAs, positive rewards work much better for these children than negative consequences.

- When consequences are necessary, natural consequences work best. (If they write on a desk, they must clean the desk. If they offend an adult or another student, a verbal or written apology is probably called for.)

- I am also a firm believer in what I call "community service." This can be a small job that the child can do in the classroom or some other part of school, either before or after school. They have violated the school community guidelines, and community service is a natural consequence. In addition, these children have a movement disorder, so sitting still for a traditional detention is nearly impossible.

- When deciding on a reward for the child to work toward, be sure to involve the child and her parents. The child must *want* the reward to work for it.
- Rewards don't have to be monetary. Get the parents to work with you by providing a reward at home also. Examples of nonmonetary rewards are:
  - A free homework pass
  - Free time to play a computer game
  - Time to go to the gym and shoot baskets
  - A prize or treat from the reward jar
  - Coupons for increments of time to watch TV or play a video game at home
  - The opportunity to go to a lower classroom or a special education class to read to the students

Again, we should always be on the lookout for things we can do *for* the child **before** the behavior begins, not things to do *to* the child **after** the behavior has occurred.

# Functional Behavioral Assessment Worksheet for a Student with Tourette Syndrome and Associated Disorders

## General Information

Student's Name                          Grade          Date

Name of Person Completing Worksheet          Position

## Behaviors Targeted to Change

The specific behavior(s) impeding learning is(are):

___ Lack of attention          ___ Out of seat frequently          ___ Verbal outbursts

___ Refusing to do work          ___ Aggressive toward others          ___ Disrespect toward adults

___ Difficulty with peers          ___ Debating issues          ___ Other*

*Other (be specific and describe what the behavior looks like)

_____

Where does the behavior occur?

___ In class          ___ Hallway between classes          ___ Working in groups

___ School bus          ___ Recess          ___ Cafeteria

Other _____

Where does the behavior *not* occur?

_____

___ In class          ___ Hallway              ___ Working in
                          between classes           groups

___ School bus        ___ Recess               ___ Cafeteria

Other _____

When does the behavior most frequently occur?

___ During      ___ During        ___ In unstructured   ___ When trying
    written         transition         environments          to start a long
    work            times                                     assignment

___ When        ___ When read-    ___ When interact-    ___ When
    taking a        ing               ing with peers        directions are
    test                                                     being given

___ When        ___ When          ___ When having       ___ Other*
    being           working in        to sit for long
    teased          groups            periods

*Other _____

As you reflect on the preceding items, which of the following might
you conclude to be possible reasons for the behaviors?

___ Interfering ___ Difficulty   ___ Stress in ___ Poor    ___ Handwrit-
    tics            with             testing       social      ing diffi-
                    transi-          situa-        skills      culties
                    tions            tions

___ Difficulty  ___ Reading      ___ Interfer- ___ Dif-    ___ Obses-
    following       deficits         ing tics      ficulty     sions that
    directions                                     remain-     are inter-
                                                   ing         fering
                                                   seated

___ Sensory     ___ Becom-       ___ Not       ___ Getting ___ Other*
    overload        ing easily       knowing       "stuck"
    in unstruc-     over-            how to
    tured envi-     whelmed          start a
    ronments                        task

*Other _____

It is always important to consider medication side effects and/or changes in medications when evaluating behaviors. Frequent communication with the school nurse and the parents is crucial.

# Summary of Functional Behavioral Assessment Worksheets

This is a summary of the information collected from all of the completed FBA worksheets to determine the reasons (function) for the behaviors observed and also which specific behaviors should be addressed when writing the positive behavior intervention plan (PBIP). This summary can be prepared by a classroom teacher, school counselor, special education teacher, administrator, or school psychologist.

## General Information

Student's Name                     Grade          Date
_____

Name of Person Completing Worksheet        Position
_____

## Behaviors Targeted to Change

1. The specific behavior(s) impeding learning is(are):

    _____

2. Where does the behavior occur?

    _____

3. Where does the behavior *not* occur?

    _____

4. When does the behavior most frequently occur?

    _____

5. As you reflect on your responses to the preceding questions, what might you conclude to be the possible reasons for the behaviors?

    _____

## Accommodations and Supports to Be Implemented

What accommodations or positive interventions are needed to decrease the likelihood of the behavior reoccurring?

___ Writing supports

___ Reduction in homework

___ Organization supports

___ Testing modifications

___ Clarifying directions

___ Peer education

___ Transition supports

___ Social skills training

___ Assistive technology

___ Assistance in reducing anxiety

___ Frequent breaks

___ More freedom of movement

___ Support in unstructured situations

___ Occupational therapy evaluation

___ Breaking down assignments, tests, and projects

List of accommodations and environmental changes that will be provided to the child in an effort to reduce the behavior(s) targeted (see Lists 4.6 through 4.9 and 4.14 for information on establishing the appropriate accommodations):

1. _____

2. _____

3. _____

4. _____

5. _____

6. _____

7. _____

8. _____

9. _____

10. _____

# Positive Behavior Intervention Plan for Student with Tourette Syndrome

## General Information

Student's Name                                    Grade        Date

Name of Person Completing Worksheet        Position

## Behaviors to Be Addressed
(never list more than three behaviors)

1. _____

2. _____

Hypothesized reasons for the behavior(s) (from item #5 of the preceding summary of the worksheets):

_____

_____

Behavioral supports to be implemented by staff:

1. _____        4. _____

2. _____        5. _____

3. _____        6. _____

Environmental changes to be implemented by staff:

1. _____        4. _____

2. _____        5. _____

3. _____        6. _____

Positive rewards to be provided to student for progress on the Positive Behavior Intervention Plan (PBIP):

At school _____

At home _____

## Communication Plan

Who will coordinate the PBIP? _____

What is the date of the next PBIP review meeting?

_____

Has every teacher and staff member working with the student received and signed the PBIP?

\_\_ Yes \_\_ No

Have the student and parents been given a copy of the FBA and agreed to the positive supports and rewards to be provided at home and at school?

\_\_ Yes \_\_ No

List the accommodations to be provided when this is shared with all the child's teachers and support staff:

1. _____

2. _____

3. _____

4. _____

5. _____

6. _____

7. _____

8. _____

9. _____

10. _____

## 4.14. Accommodations for
## Associated Disorders

*Sensory issues* are often the cause of behaviors at school, at home, and in the community. These behaviors are most likely to occur in an environment of sensory overload such as:

- Hallways between classes
- The school bus
- The cafeteria
- Assemblies
- The playground
- Physical education class

Here are some accommodations that may assist in these environments:

- Allow the child to leave class three to four minutes early to avoid crowded hallways. Allow him to bring a friend so that he can have social time as other students do.
- Find a quiet place for him to eat lunch with a couple of friends.
- During school assemblies, allow the child to sit at the end of the row, preferably toward the back so if the assembly gets too noisy he can easily step out to the hallway for a few minutes.
- Allow him to sit up front on the school bus so the driver can keep an eye on him and prevent potential problems.
  - Some children do better on a small school bus with fewer students.
  - The school bus ride at the end of the day can be particularly problematic because the child is already tired and on overload.
- On the playground or in PE class, keep an aide nearby who can help the child remove himself before a problem escalates.

- Allow the child to wear a headset in noisy, chaotic environments.
- Involve the school's occupational therapist to assess sensory needs and suggest possible solutions.

OCD can cause kids to become stuck and have difficulty switching gears cognitively:

- They tend to melt down during transition times or when there is any change in the day's routine.
- These children also may have what I call an "obsessive sense of justice," meaning they will become very upset if they believe there has been an injustice.
- Their behavior frequently resembles that of stubborn children who just want their own way.

Following are some suggestions to accommodate these children and prevent behaviors:

- Transition warnings are essential—tell them, for example, "In five minutes, we will be changing activities." "In three minutes, we will be having dinner." If they are still not satisfied that they have completed what they have been working on to perfection, allow them to arrange a specific time when they can come back and finish it.
- A student with an obsession to count the words on every line she reads may need to listen to books on tape.
- A student with a germ obsession can be encouraged to carry antiseptic hand wipes or antibacterial cleaner in her pocket to wash her hands whenever she feels "contaminated."
- A student who can't write without a perfectly sharpened pencil and is always at the pencil sharpener can be given a jar of sharpened pencils at the beginning of each class or a mechanical pencil.

- A student with a symmetry obsession may constantly erase and rewrite her work because it "doesn't look right." Allowing the student to use a computer for written work can alleviate this problem.
- Provide supports that reduce stress.
  - Anxiety is often an issue for students with OCD.
  - School must be a place where it is safe to make mistakes.
  - Punishing or ridiculing children only serves to increase anxiety and the difficulties associated with it.
- If there is going to be a substitute teacher or a change in schedule for the day, let the child know right away in the morning or the day before, if possible.
- Distraction can be a good way to break an obsession that a child is stuck on.
  - Change to a new environment.
  - Allow the student some physical activity to help redirect the obsession.
- Humor can be a great tool to help kids get unstuck.
- When they feel they must debate an issue, allow them to make their point briefly and validate that they may have a point (even if you don't agree with them).
  - Establish a nonverbal signal with the child in advance that indicates that you want to discuss his concern with him, but it needs to be done after class so it's not disruptive.
  - If he can let it go until after class, establish a reward that he will receive for doing so.
  - Avoid power struggles. They only escalate a bad situation.
- Remain composed and speak in a calm, nonemotional voice when attempting to redirect the child.
- Some kids who suffer from anxiety may need to call home two or three times a day to ensure that their parents are OK. They

may need to sit near the classroom door or carry a cell phone in their pocket to reduce anxiety.

- Creativity may be your greatest asset when working with kids with OCD and anxiety. You must first assess what the difficulty is:
  - Children are often reluctant to disclose their obsessions and compulsions, for fear that people will think they are crazy (because they feel crazy).
  - It is the professionals' role to help children feel comfortable disclosing what they are obsessing about.
  - Look for red flags (discussed in full in List 1.20):
    - Writing and erasing
    - Constant pencil sharpening
    - Inability to turn assignments in
    - Perfectionistic tendencies
    - Asking repeated questions
    - Difficulty transitioning
  - Communication with the parents is also essential because, as with tics, the obsessions wax and wane.

*Dysgraphia* is a very common comorbid learning disability for children with TS and OCD. It can put enormous stress on children because they may be unable to write quickly and neatly, copy things correctly, or take class notes.

Both motor tics and obsessions can also interfere with children's ability to write. Some possible accommodations include:

- Occupational therapy (OT) intervention
  - OT and physical therapy support might be helpful with handwriting difficulties, but as the child gets older, the therapies are much less effective. Use of these therapies is best determined on a case-by-case basis.

- Provide alternatives for tests, assignments, reports, and such:
  - Tests can be given orally or using a tape recorder.
  - Waive or ease time limits on tests.
  - Standardized test answers can be written directly in the test booklet and transferred onto the answer sheet by a teacher or an assistant.
  - Reports can be delivered orally or on tape.
  - The use of a computer or word processor is often a critical accommodation.
  - For younger students, a scribe may be necessary until they are more proficient keyboarders.
- Don't penalize students for poor handwriting.
- Don't penalize them for spelling errors and encourage the use of spell-checking software.
- Shorten or consolidate assignments:
  - Assign ten math problems instead of twenty.
  - The *quality* of the assignment is most important, not the *quantity*.
- Verify that all homework assignments are copied down accurately.
- Provide graph paper to help line up math problems or allow the child to turn the paper sideways.
- Provide class notes rather than having the student copy from the chalkboard or overhead.
  - Some schools have a computer program called Blackboard that allows teachers to post all class notes for students to download.
  - The student can use the class notes to highlight while the teacher is talking.
- Photocopy materials, rather than requiring the student to copy them. This approach is especially important when assigning math homework.

- If photocopying is not possible, allow a parent or teacher's aide to copy the problems. The math calculations are important, not the ability to copy problems.

- Encourage the use of an index card to visually track the page during reading assignments.

- The use of a calculator for math can circumvent visual-motor difficulties.

- Allow extra time for written work.

- Scan homework and tests into a computer.

- Allow the student to use a cell phone or digital camera to take a picture of the assignment on the board rather than trying to copy it.

- Voice-activated computer software such as Dragon Speak Naturally can be a huge help to children (developed and sold by Nuance; www.nuance.com/dragon/index.htm). Now available as a free app on iPods and iPads.

- Request an assistive technology evaluation to investigate what software is available to assist children with written expression and handwriting deficits.

  - Software is available for scanning worksheets and the like into a computer.

  - Look into mind-mapping software such as Inspirations that helps children who have difficulty with written expression (www.inspiration.com).

*Auditory Processing Deficits*

- Have the child tested by an audiologist or speech language pathologist
- Reduce background noise
- Have the child repeat and/or rephrase directions
- Speak at a slightly slower rate
- Use simple expressive sentences

- Use visuals
- Allow extra time for responses
- Use preferential seating
- Let the child wear a headset when doing independent work to block out background noise

*Executive Dysfunction*

Children with executive dysfunction have a difficult time with anything that involves organization. They lose everything, don't write down their homework assignments, and come to class unprepared. They will always need accommodations to help them to be successful in school. These could include:

- Place them in a structured but flexible classrooms.
- Break down assignments.
  - Hand the child only one paper at a time, rather than several.
  - Break down all long-range assignments and projects into shorter, more manageable parts—for example, Part One is due in two days, rather than the entire project being due in three weeks.
- Reduce the length of homework assignments: quality is the important thing, not quantity.
- Provide a daily assignment sheet (agenda) to be filled out by the student and verified or initialed by the teacher.
- Ask parents to verify that all the work is accomplished and assist with homework prioritizing and management.
- Allow the student to leave the last class a little early in order to pack up and organize materials.
  - The student will have a little more time to be at her locker without the distractions of a crowded hallway.
  - An adult's assistance may also be necessary.
- Provide an extra set of textbooks for use at home.

- Color-code textbook covers, notebooks, and folders—the blue folder goes with the blue science book.

- Keep a supply of paper, pens, and pencils to lend to students who forget or constantly lose such things.

- Don't penalize a student who forgets or loses basic classroom supplies. Make arrangements with parents to "resupply" the missing materials.

- To make sure you get supplies back at the end of class, take something of the student's as "hostage"—have them leave one shoe near your desk during class that they can reclaim when the supply is returned.

- Teach children basic study skills and organizational strategies:
  - How to sequence and break down tasks into more manageable segments
  - How to prioritize for better time management using, for example, an index card for each assignment

- Structure assignments:
  - Make lists of items that can be crossed off when the student has completed each assignment
  - For longer assignments, provide frequent breaks.

- Give the student a "word bank" to select from on fill-in-the-blank tests.

- Establish a method of daily communication between home and school through an assignment book or e-mail.

- Assign a "homework buddy" for the child to call on for help with such matters as "What was the assignment?" and "When is the paper due?"

- Post a schedule of the day's activities in front of the class or on the child's desk, so that nothing comes as a surprise or is unexpected.

- Allow students to e-mail their completed assignments to the teacher so they don't get lost.

- Allow students to save their work on a thumb drive to be printed out at school.
- Students with executive dysfunction do much better using a three-ring binder or Trapper Keeper in which all folders can be kept together. The Trapper Keeper can be zipped to ensure that materials are not lost.
  - Organize the folders in the binder by each day's class schedule.
  - Keep a zippered, three-hole-punched pouch in the binder and fill it with lots of extra supplies.
  - Check the pouch frequently and replenish when necessary.
  - Be sure to put hole reinforcements in the binder to maintain and repair torn papers.
  - Keep a separate folder just for homework that has been completed. The student is less apt to lose completed assignments if they are all kept together.
- Weekly folder, backpack, and locker cleanouts may be necessary and can be part of resource room time.
- Assigning the student two lockers can be a helpful strategy. One locker can be used for coat and gym clothes, and the other for books and folders.
- Some students do better in the classroom with two desks or a big table where they can organize their belongings and spread them out.
- Allow these students to leave the last class early to e-mail their assignments home to themselves from the resource room, guidance office, or school library.
- Some students prefer to call their home answering machines and read their assignments into the machine.
- Take advantage of any system the school may have to list all assignments on the school's web page.

# Social Skills Interventions for Students with TS and/or OCD

### Social Skills Training

- In a school setting, several people are available to do social skills training: the speech language pathologist, the social worker, the school psychologist, or the school counselor.
- This training is often a very important service for children with TS and OCD and can be included on their individualized education program (IEP).
- Social skills groups can be the best way to accomplish social skills training. Because this is a social deficit, including the child in a lunch group or a before-school or after-school group can be crucial.

### Use of Social Stories

- Social stories are a great tool to use both by school personnel working with these children as well as parents in the home environment.
- Many social stories are available, and two of the best-known series are by Carol Gray (www.thegraycenter.org) and Michelle Garcia (www.socialthinking.com). You can also do a web search on "social stories" to find other available series.

Over the course of my time spent with children with these neurological disorders, I have observed that many of them are socially and emotionally immature. They frequently exhibit behaviors resembling those of children two-thirds of their chronological age. When we keep this propensity in mind, it becomes easier to understand and work with these children.

# Section Five

## OTHER HELPFUL CHECKLISTS FOR PARENTS AND TEACHERS

5.1.   Educational Rights of Students with TS and OCD

5.2.   Individuals with Disabilities Education Act (IDEA)

5.3.   What Is a 504 Accommodation Plan?

5.4.   Requesting Services

5.5.   Sample Physician's Letter

5.6.   How to Proceed If You Disagree with the School's Evaluation

5.7.   Being a Role Model for Children with TS or OCD and Their Peers

5.8.   Relaxation Techniques

5.9.   School Placement

5.10.  Sources of Help and Support

5.11.  Recommended Organizations, Web Sites, Books, Videos, Articles, and Brochures

## 5.1. Educational Rights of Students with TS and OCD

What are the options? Two federal laws govern the services for which your child may be eligible: the Americans with Disabilities Act and the Individuals with Disabilities Education Act.

### Americans with Disabilities Act (ADA)

The American with Disabilities Act (ADA) levels the playing field for students with disabilities by providing educational accommodations through a 504 plan, named for section 504 of the ADA. (See List 5.3 for more specific information on Section 504.)

*Examples of Possible Accommodations Under a 504 Plan*

- Extended time on tests and assignments
- Testing in a separate location
- Extra set of textbooks at home
- Preferential seating
- Access to a computer for long written assignments
- In-service on TS for all staff working with the child
- Extra locker to assist with organization
- Use of a scribe
- Access to books on tape

## 5.2. Individuals with Disabilities Education Act (IDEA)

The Individuals with Disabilities Act (IDEA) provides an individualized education plan (IEP)—accommodations plus direct services of a special education teacher or other service providers (such as occupational therapists, speech therapists, and counselors).

*How Do I Know Whether My Child Might Need Services?*

- Decline in grades
- Increased frustration
- Decrease in the child's self-esteem
- Social difficulties
- A negative attitude about school
- School avoidance or phobia
- Behavioral issues at school
- Increase in TS symptoms due to stress or anxiety
- Difficulties at home that are a direct result of school issues

*How Does My Child Qualify for an IEP under IDEA?*

- An IEP team must determine whether the disability interferes with a student's academic performance and functioning significantly enough to warrant an IEP.

- It is *performance*, not *ability*, that must be "significantly impacted." While some of the aptitude scores may indicate that a student is very capable, his grades in class may not be commensurate with his ability. Therefore, it can be logically reasoned that the disability does have a significant impact on performance.

- While the major focus of school is academic success, schools are also responsible for the physical, emotional, and functional development of their students. Children's social and emotional well-being also need to be considered.

## Section 300.324 of IDEA: Development, Review, and Revision of IEP

(1) *General.* In developing each child's IEP, the IEP Team must consider:

(iv) The academic, developmental, and functional needs of the child.

## A Word to the Wise

### Do Not Accept a Refusal for Classification That Is Based on the Following Reasons

- Your child does not qualify as Learning Disabled (LD). Because TS is a health condition, you are not seeking a classification of LD, but Other Health Impaired (OHI), so the LD designation does not apply. (Full discussion of IDEA follows in the next section.)

- Your child does not qualify for services because he is receiving good grades or is not failing. Federal law states that special education cannot be denied because a student is receiving passing grades and/or progressing from grade to grade. Additionally, the law states that a student's developmental and functional progress must be taken into consideration in addition to academic performance.

## IDEA

In 2004 the federal act that governs the services that children with disabilities receive—the Individuals with Disabilities Education Act (IDEA)—was reauthorized. To our great delight, for the first time Tourette Syndrome was officially listed as a disability under the category of Other Health Impaired. The section of IDEA that covers TS is section 300.8 (c) (9), and it reads as follows:

> ## IDEA 2004 and Federal Regulations 300.8 (c) (9)
>
> We believe that Tourette Syndrome is commonly misunderstood to be a behavioral or emotional condition, rather than a neurological condition. Therefore including TS in the definition of OHI (Other Health Impaired) may help correct the misconception of TS as a behavioral or conduct disorder and prevent the misdiagnosis of their needs.

Why is this an important accomplishment for individuals with TS and associated disorders?

- Before this provision was added, very few states had TS listed by name as a disability under IDEA.
- Children with TS across the country were commonly denied services because they did not exhibit a specific learning disability.
- Many children with TS were wrongly classified as either Emotionally Disturbed or Behaviorally Disturbed, both of which are inappropriate classifications in these cases.
- The classification often determines which services are provided, so if a child is inappropriately classified, she could end up in the wrong placement and receive services that are inappropriate and do not meet her needs.
- Tourette Syndrome is a health impairment and should be classified as such.

Does this mean that every child with TS will be classified Other Health Impaired and receive an individualized education plan (IEP)?

- No, but once a physician makes the diagnosis and it is shown that the disorder affects the child's academic performance, learning, functioning, and/or social and emotional well-being, the child will receive services and be appropriately classified as Other Health Impaired (OHI).
- The complexity of TS and all its associated disorders make it relatively easy to show the impact of the disorder, for example:
  - Tics can be very interfering to the completion of work.
  - OCD can also interfere with tasks that need to be completed.
  - Dysgraphia makes it impossible for children to write, take notes, and perform essential academic tasks.
  - Executive dysfunction is one of the most common reasons for children to need assistance in a school setting.
  - ADHD symptoms can also be very debilitating.

The most important thing to remember is that most children with TS have several other comorbid neurological disorders, and even if some of them are relatively mild, the coexistence of all these disorders can create academic and emotional havoc for a child.

## 5.3. What Is a 504 Accommodation Plan?

A 504 Accommodation Plan falls under the auspices of the Americans with Disabilities Act (ADA). This federal act was first authorized in 1973 and states: "No otherwise qualified individual with a disability in the United States .†.†. shall solely by reason of her or his disability, be excluded from the participation in, be denied the benefits of, or be subjected to discrimination under any program or activity receiving Federal financial assistance" (http://ed.gov/about/offices/list/ocr/504faq.html). The intent of Section 504 has always been to provide "equal access" to a free and appropriate education so that students with disabilities are not discriminated against due to the symptoms of their disabilities.

Section 504 was amended in 2008. The amendment "emphasizes that the definition of disability should be construed in favor of broad coverage of individuals to the maximum extent permitted by the terms of the ADA and generally shall not require extensive analysis."

- The amendment restores the original definition of disability intended by Congress in that the disability "substantially" limits a major life activity—instead of "significantly" or "severely" limiting activity—as has been mistakenly used.

- The 2008 amendment also "clarifies that an impairment that is episodic or in remission is a disability if it would substantially limit a major life activity when active" (http://www.access-board.gov/about/laws/ada-amendments.htm).

- This is particularly pertinent to students with TS and OCD, since symptoms of both of these disorders wax and wane.

- A major life activity can include reading, writing, communication, learning, attending, or movement.

- A 504 Plan, however, provides *only accommodations* and not direct services.

Can children with TS do just as well with a 504 Accommodation Plan as they would with an IEP?

- Some students with TS function well with just a 504 Accommodation Plan.
- Many students will need the direct services of a special education teacher, physical therapist, occupational therapist, speech language therapist, or other support services provided only in an IEP to be successful in school.
- Each child is an individual, and his TS symptoms—as well as the severity of all associated disorders—must be taken into consideration when deciding which level of services will best meet the needs of that child.
- The most important thing to remember is that *students with TS and associated disorders are entitled to services under Section 504 of the ADA or appropriate classification of OHI under the IDEA.*

## 5.4. Requesting Services

When requesting services, a letter of diagnosis from the treating physician is required, because you are requesting a classification of Other Health Impaired (OHI). You are trying to prove that TS and the associated neurological disorders are affecting the child's academic performance, learning, functioning, and/or social and emotional well-being. The treating physician also needs to address specifically how these disorders are having these effects. If the child is seeing an outside therapist, a similar letter from that person would also be in order.

The letter needs to be very specific, addressing, but not limited to, the following items:

- Particular interfering tics and obsessions
- Anxiety issues
- Attention deficits
- Handwriting issues
- Behavioral issues at home and at school
- Social and emotional issues
- Disorganization

List 5.5 shows a sample physician's letter that parents and/or the school can share with the doctor involved. Doctors don't always know how to formulate a letter to the school for the purpose of obtaining services. This is not their area of expertise, and they are usually very willing to refer to such a sample letter.

## 5.5. Sample Physician's Letter

### Sample Letter from the Treating Physician

To Whom It May Concern:

_____ is currently under my care and has been diagnosed with *[Tourette Syndrome, ADHD, OCD, or other]*. All of these disorders are having a negative impact on his/her school performance as well as his/her social and emotional well-being. The following tics and obsessions *[be specific]* that he/she is currently exhibiting are interfering with the ability to *[read, write, and complete assignments in a timely fashion]*. The symptomology of *[Tourette Syndrome, ADHD, OCD, or other]* is also proving to impact negatively on his/her academic performance. He/She is unable to organize materials appropriately, is very distracted by external stimuli, cannot complete assignments on time, is getting into trouble because of his/her impulsivity, and is under great stress socially because of the nature of his/her tics. Issues at home with homework completion appear to be causing frequent meltdowns.

It is my recommendation that a full battery of psychoeducational testing be administered by the school and/or by an outside neuropsychologist to test for the following disabilities, which are very commonly seen in children diagnosed with these disorders:

- Dysgraphia

- Sensory processing deficits

- Auditory processing disorder

- Language processing deficits

- Memory deficits

- Executive dysfunction

*(continued)*

(continued)

_____ is also currently taking the following medications, which may be affecting his/her ability to attend properly in the classroom. I will be available for further consultation once the testing process has been completed to assist in making specific recommendations for an IEP.

Thank you.

Sincerely,

_____

## 5.6. How to Proceed If You Disagree with the School's Evaluation

If parents believe that their child's educational difficulties have not been properly identified or appropriately assessed by the school's evaluation, they can request an outside independent evaluation from a professional who specializes in neurological disorders—a neuropsychologist, occupational therapist, speech language therapist, or audiologist.

According to the Individuals with Disabilities Education Act (IDEA), the school has two choices:

- To provide the funding for the outside evaluation
- To take the parents to a hearing

Following are the federal regulations from IDEA that govern this topic:

§ 300.103.(b) Parent right to evaluation at public expense.

1. A parent has the right to an independent educational evaluation at public expense if the parent disagrees with an evaluation obtained by the public agency (school district), subject to the conditions in paragraphs (b)(2) through (4) of this section.

2. If a parent requests an independent educational evaluation at public expense, the public agency must, without unnecessary delay, either:

   i. File a due process complaint to request a hearing to show that its evaluation is appropriate; or

   ii. Ensure that an independent educational evaluation is provided at public expense, unless the agency demonstrates in a hearing pursuant to §§ 300.507 through 300.513 that the evaluation obtained by the parent did not meet agency criteria.

3. If the public agency files a due process complaint notice to request a hearing and the final decision is that the agency's

evaluation is appropriate, the parent still has the right to an independent educational evaluation, but not at public expense.

4. If a parent requests an independent educational evaluation, the public agency may ask for the parent's reason why he or she objects to the public evaluation. However, the public agency may not require the parent to provide an explanation and may not unreasonably delay either providing the independent educational evaluation at public expense or filing a due process complaint to request a due process hearing to defend the public evaluation.

5. A parent is entitled to only one independent educational evaluation at public expense each time the public agency conducts an evaluation with which the parent disagrees.

However, the school is *only* obligated to take the independent evaluations into "consideration." It is not obligated to follow the evaluator's recommendations.

## 5.7. Being a Role Model for Children with TS or OCD and Their Peers

There is nothing more important for parents and educators than being a positive role model for their children and students. In a classroom setting, teachers, counselors, and aides are the role models for other children's treatment of and reaction to a child with TS or OCD. If teachers or parents treat him differently and separate him from other students, it gives permission to other students and siblings to do the same.

Setting an example of acceptance and tolerance of the differences in all students is one of the most important lessons we will ever teach our children. As an educator, I have always tried to live my professional teaching career by this wonderful quote from the great child psychologist Haim Ginott. It was posted in my classroom for thirty-one years.

> I've come to the conclusion that I am the decisive element in the classroom. It's my personal approach that creates the climate. It's my daily mood that makes the weather. As a teacher, I possess a tremendous power to make a child's life miserable or joyous. I can be a tool of torture or an instrument of inspiration. I can humiliate or honor, hurt or heal. In all situations, it is my response that decides whether a crisis will be escalated or deescalated and a child humanized or dehumanized.
>
> —Haim Ginott

## 5.8. Relaxation Techniques

It is commonly known that stress increases tics, obsessions, and anxiety, as well as other aspects of these disorders. All of the following practices will serve to relax the individual and will thus help decrease symptoms:

- Exercise and frequent breaks in school.
- Allowing the student to have a relaxation break before starting homework each night.
- When the student is deeply involved in an activity she really enjoys, tics often diminish significantly or go away entirely.
- Some children find relaxation in listening to music, playing video games, playing a sport, reading, watching TV, or playing a musical instrument. Each child is an individual, and we therefore should focus on what helps relax that individual.
- Some people find activities such as yoga, meditation, and biofeedback very calming and choose these options to help relax and thereby calm down symptoms.

## 5.9. School Placement

- Most children with TS or OCD are placed in a regular classroom setting, where their disorders can easily be accommodated.

- Many will benefit greatly from a cotaught class—with a special education teacher and a regular education teacher in the same classroom—or from a period in the resource room each day.

- Motor and vocal tics should *never* be a reason for removing a child from a mainstream classroom.

- Some children, because of the severity of their associated disorders, will require placement in a self-contained classroom setting where more supports are available.

- Frequently it is the specific learning disabilities and/or the severity of the ADHD that make it necessary to place a child in a more restrictive environment.

- Each child is an individual, and *all* of his needs must be evaluated before placement is determined.

- Although these children may appear to have significant behavior problems, a class for children with emotional disturbances is *not* an appropriate placement.

- Behaviors for these children have a neurological base, which is very different from behaviors with an emotional base. The same techniques don't work for these children. (See Lists 1.18, 4.12, and 4.13 for an in-depth discussion of behavior.)

"How you explain why a child is doing poorly, leads directly to what you are going to do about it."

–Ross W. Greene, author of *The Explosive Child* and *Lost at School* and publisher, www.livesinthebalance.org

## 5.10. Sources of Help and Support

Educators and parents should seek out any supports available in their community to assist them in working with children with TS or OCD. There are Tourette Syndrome Association chapters across the country, as well as independent state organizations that provide a multitude of services and materials on TS, OCD, and all the associated disorders for families and professionals dealing with TS. (Also see List 5.11 for more recommended organizations and resources.)

- The national OCD Foundation provides wonderful services for families dealing with OCD.
- There are many local OCD affiliates across the country.
- All of these organizations can assist in finding appropriate medical and allied professional referrals in your area.

## 5.11. Recommended Organizations, Web Sites, Books, Videos, Articles, and Brochures

### Organization Web Sites

Tourette Syndrome Association

www.tsa-usa.org

Obsessive Compulsive Foundation

www.ocfoundation.org

Pennsylvania Tourette Syndrome Alliance

www.patsainc.org

TICS of Georgia

www.georgiatourette.org

Joshua Center for Neurological Disorders (Kansas City, Mo.)

www.joshuacenter.com

New Jersey Center for Tourette Syndrome

www.njcts.org

Council for Exceptional Children

www.cec.sped.org

Children and Adults with Attention Deficit/Hyperactivity
   Disorder

www.chadd.org

Attention Deficit Disorder Association

www.add.org

Learning Disabilities Association of America

www.ldanatl.org

National Center for Learning Disabilities

www.ncld.org

National Information Clearinghouse for Handicapped Children
   and Youth

www.nichcy.org

Parent Advocacy Center for Educational Rights

www.pacer.org

Parent Training and Information Centers

www.taalliance.org

## Books, Nonfiction

*Children with Tourette Syndrome: A Parents' Guide,* 2nd ed., by Tracy Lynne Marsh (Bethesda, Md.: Woodbine House, 2007).

*Search for the Tourette Syndrome and Human Behavior Genes,* by David E. Comings (Duarte, Calif.: Hope Press, 1990).

*A Mind of Its Own: Tourette's Syndrome–A Story and a Guide,* by Ruth Dowling Bruun (New York: Oxford University Press, 1994).

*Twitch and Shout: A Touretter's Tale,* by Lowell Handler (New York: Penguin, 1998).

*Tourette Syndrome,* by Donald J. Cohen, Joseph Jankovics, and Christopher Goetz (Philadelphia: Lippincott Williams & Wilkins, 2001).

*Tourette's Syndrome: Tics, Obsessions, Compulsions–Developmental Psychopathology and Clinical Care,* by James Leckman and Donald Cohen (New York: Wiley, 1999).

*Tictionary: A Reference Guide to the World of Tourette Syndrome, Asperger Syndrome, Attention Deficit Hyperactivity Disorder, and Obsessive Compulsive Disorder for Parents and Professionals,* by Becky Ottinger and Frederick Engh (Overland Park, Kans.: Autism Asperger Publishing, 2003).

*The Explosive Child,* by Ross Greene (New York: Harper Collins, 2005).

*Treating Tourette Syndrome and Tic Disorders: A Guide for Practitioners,* Douglas W. Woods, John T. Walkup, and John C. Piacentini, eds. (New York: Guilford, 2007).

*Tics and Tourette's: A Patient and Family Guide–Breakthrough Discoveries in Natural Treatments,* by Shelia J. Rogers (Broken Arrow, Okla.: Association for Comprehensive NeuroTherapy, 2005).

*The Out-of-Sync Child,* by Carol Stock Kranowitz (New York: Skylight Press/ Perigee, 2005). (For children with sensory issues)

### Sensory Issues

*Front of the Class,* by Brad Cohen and Lisa Wysocky (New York: St. Martin's Griffin, 2008).

*Executive Skills in Children and Adolescents: A Practical Guide to Assessment and Intervention,* by Peg Dawson Eddy (New York: Guilford, 2003).

*Here's the Deal, Don't Touch Me* (OCD), by Howie Mandel (New York: Bantam, 2009).

## Books, Fiction

*Hi, I'm Adam: A Child's Book About Tourette Syndrome*, by Adam Behrens (Duarte, Calif.: Hope Press, 1990).

*Adam and the Magic Marble* (for children), by Adam Behrens (Duarte, Calif.: Hope Press, 1991).

*Against Medical Advice*, by James Patterson and Hal Friedman (New York: Little, Brown, 2008).

*QUIT IT*, by Marcia Byalick (New York: Yearling, 2004).

*A Test of Will*, by Diane Shader Smith (self-published, 2002).

*Icy Sparks*, by Gwen Hyman Rubio (New York: Penguin, 2001).

*Motherless Brooklyn*, by Jonathan Lethem (New York: Vintage, 2000).

*Erika's Little Secret* (for children), by Candida Koran (Bayside, N.Y.: Tourette Syndrome Association, 2008).

## Videos

*I Have Tourette's, but Tourette's Doesn't Have Me* (HBO Network, 2005); wonderful for a peer in-service.

*A Teacher Looks at Tourette Syndrome* (Tourette Syndrome Association); an educator's in-service DVD.

## Brochures

*Bus Drivers Need to Understand the Difficulties of Tourette Syndrome*, by Stephen Babcock (School Transportation News, 2008).

*Teachers Who "Get It,"* by Candida B. Korman (Tourette Syndrome Association, 2009).

*Advocating for an Aide*, by Kathleen Giordano (Tourette Syndrome Association, 2006).

*Tips for School Meetings*, by Kathleen Giordano (Tourette Syndrome Association, 2007).

*It's Not Just the Tics: Classroom Learning and Behavioral Issues with Tourette Syndrome*, by Linda Abbott, Barbara Baron, and Louise Kiessling (Neurodevelopmental Center, MHRI, 2001).

*Guide for Paraprofessionals Working with Students with TS*, by Kathleen Giordano (Tourette Syndrome Association, 2007).

*R.A.G.E.: Repeated Anger Generated Episodes*, by Cathy Budman (Tourette Syndrome Association, 1999).

## Brochures and Articles by Susan Conners

"Tourette Syndrome and Associated Disorders in the Classroom," by Susan Conners, *Council for Exceptional Children Newsletter*, 2009, 27(2).

*The IEP for Students with Tourette Syndrome: A Parent's Handbook*, by Susan Conners (Tourette Syndrome Association, 2004).

*The IEP for Students with Tourette Syndrome: An Educator's Guide*, by Susan Conners (Tourette Syndrome Association, 2004).

*Understanding and Dealing with Vocal Tics in the Classroom*, by Susan Conners (Tourette Syndrome Association, 2010).

*Section 504, the Americans with Disabilities Act, Versus the Individuals with Disabilities Education Act: What Is the Difference?* by Susan Conners (Tourette Syndrome Association, 2007).

*Bullying and Tourette Syndrome*, by Susan Conners (Tourette Syndrome Association, 2007).

*TS and OT*, by Susan Conners (Tourette Syndrome Association, 2007).

"Tourette Syndrome in the Classroom," by Susan Conners, *Communiqué: The Official Magazine of the National Association of School Psychologists*, 2002, 31.

"Susan Conners: An Educator's Observations About Living with and Educating Others About Tourette's Syndrome," *Intervention in School and Clinic*, 2003, 39, 99–108.

# Appendix: Real-Life Scenarios

As I have stated over and over throughout the pages of this book, Tourette Syndrome and obsessive-compulsive disorder are two of the most challenging disorders that you will ever work with in your classroom. Not only do children with these disorders exhibit bizarre symptoms that frequently look more like behaviors than symptoms of a neurological disorder, but they almost all have other comorbid neurological disorders that complicate the situation. Your best asset in dealing with children with all these disorders is *creativity*. As much as I dislike the expression "thinking outside the box," this is absolutely what we must do with all these disorders. Many times we haven't been able to come to terms with the fact that the child can't stop doing what she is doing.

The anecdotal stories related in this section are all events in which I have been personally involved, all of which took collaboration, communication, and, most important, creativity. One of the key people who can help resolve these difficult situations is the child. Each of these stories is about a real child who was able to work with us to help come up with an accommodation (as strange as it may have seemed) to help him overcome a problem and be socially and academically successful. He may very well be the key to helping you, the reader, truly understand what works. I thank all these children for allowing me to use their stories, even when their names have been changed. The knowledge and insight that have allowed me to help these children and write this book have come from the children themselves. They are to be commended, thanked, admired, and applauded for their courage, strength, and insight into the baffling disorders that they live with every day.

# Motor and Vocal Tics

## Tap, Tap, Tap

A child with Tourette Syndrome (TS) developed an annoying hand tic, which caused him to feel the need to tap a pencil in one spot on his desk. The constant tap, tap, tapping was, of course, very distracting to others. The teacher, thinking creatively, brought in a large, flat sponge, and she and the student with TS taped it to the desk. The symptom was "accommodated." The child's tic wasn't ridiculed or punished, but instead the noise was softened, and the disruption to the teacher and classmates was greatly reduced.

## "I Have a Chicken in My Pants"

A seventh grader with TS (we'll call him Chris) suddenly developed a vocal tic that involved shouting three or four times during a class period, "I have a chicken in my pants." The first time it occurred, teachers were perplexed as to what to do. Having TS myself, I admit to having a bit of a warped sense of humor about the strange symptoms that suddenly pop up. I've also been a teacher for thirty-three years. The first inclination of most staff members was to tell Chris that this was not appropriate and to ask him to leave the room before he said it. After a few minutes of thought, I knew this plan wouldn't work. First, unfortunately, people with TS don't usually sense the tic far enough in advance to be able to leave the room before it happens. Second, I could envision this child spending most of the class time trying to anticipate the tic and then leaving the room in anticipation. Imagine how this would interfere with his ability to concentrate on the lesson, to say nothing of the time spent out of the classroom.

My suggestion consisted of two steps. First, I asked the teachers to keep track of the number of interruptions that occurred during one class period on one day. They were to count all interruptions—sneezing, coughing, nose blowing, pencil sharpening, chairs scraping, things dropping, intercoms blaring, and planes flying over the school. I asked them to compare the number of these interruptions with Chris shouting three or four times, "I have a chicken in my pants." His repeated declaration paled in comparison to all the other daily interruptions to which they had become accustomed. The second step involved explaining to the other students (with the permission of Chris and his parents) what TS was and why Chris said what he did. With everyone's agreement, a peer inservice was held. The other students and teachers were used to and understood all the other interruptions. Now Chris became just one of all the other interruptions. He can now tell us endlessly about the chicken in his pants and no one even raises an eyebrow. Attitude and knowledge are everything. And the chicken lived happily ever after.

## PB and J

A fifth grader from Florida developed two very difficult tics. The first was a motor tic that involved jerking her leg forward with great force while sitting at her desk at school. The leg would hit the metal rung of the desk, which would then cause her shoe to fly off. Other students in the class would have to dodge the flying shoe, retrieve it, and bring it back to her. As you can imagine, it became a significant disruption to the class. More important, I noticed that she was doing a lot of damage to her leg as she hit it against the desk. My suggestion was for the teachers to allow her to put her shoes on the shelf on the side of the classroom as soon as she came in. It solved the problem. I also asked them to put gauze around her leg and the rung of her desk so that her leg would be protected.

Her second difficult tic was shouting out "peanut butter" four or five times a class period. Since the other students had not been educated about TS, they were becoming increasingly annoyed with this. Some even admitted to being afraid of her because of these bizarre behaviors. Once the class had been educated, instead of showing annoyance, every time she said "peanut butter" the other students would simply say "jelly." Problem solved!

## The Dreaded Cursing

A young man attended a school with a very large population of Native American students. Each time one of these students would call any attention to themselves, this boy would yell out "spear chucker."

A high school student had many tics in this category. She was actually asked to leave school because of these vocalizations and spent most of an academic year on home instruction. As she was walking down the hall, she passed another female student who was wearing a very inappropriate outfit. The top was clearly too low cut, and the skirt was too short. As she passed her, the girl with TS yelled out "whore."

Every time a fourth grader in Wisconsin saw the school principal, she would yell out, "Kill the principal," followed by "Kill the #$%& principal." She was a very sweet, bright child, but that was her tic at the moment.

A sixth grader suddenly developed a tic that involved shouting out "I had sex last night." Although the school was aware that he had TS, Child Protective Services (CPS) was called by school personnel, which thrust the family into a CPS investigation that went on for months.

Of course, the only solution to all of these issues was simply educating every adult and student who came into contact with that student. One school, with the parents' permission, was very proactive and actually posted a sign in the main office that read as follows:

### Notice to Visitors

We have a child here at our school who is a wonderful young man, but who has a medical condition called Tourette Syndrome. You may hear noises, inappropriate comments, or profanity coming from this child. Please ignore these symptoms. This is a neurological condition, and he is unable to control it. If you have any questions or concerns, please feel free to speak with a staff member. We appreciate your kindness and compassion.

–The Administration

One seventh-grade boy named Joe developed a vocal tic over the summer months that involved shouting out "you ass." He was very concerned about returning to school with this propensity, so he became quite creative and began instead saying "you ass A." By just adding the A it now sounded like "USA" and was much more acceptable. (Unfortunately, the tic eventually changed to "dumb ass" which was much harder to camouflage.)

## Head, Shoulders, Knees, and Toes

When a twelve-year-old boy met someone for the first time, he had to touch her wrist, her elbow, and her shoulder, in that order. This was clearly a complex motor tic. He also had to do this to students that he accidentally bumped into in the hallways. Imagine the difficulty this boy must have with other seventh graders whom he has to touch in this fashion. The solution was to allow him to leave each class four minutes early with a friend while the halls were empty, thus reducing the number of people he bumped into.

## Where Should Jeannie Sit?

One young girl named Jeannie had a twirling tic, which caused her to have to stand up multiple times a day next to her desk and twirl a few times. When I observed the class, the teacher related that this tic was causing a lot of difficulty in the classroom. I immediately figured out why. Her desk was in the center of the classroom. Not only was this a disruption, but I could see that it was very embarrassing to Jeannie. We immediately moved her desk to the side of the room, so that the other students barely noticed when she twirled.

## No Applause Necessary

A sixth grader suddenly developed a clapping tic. He would put his pen or pencil down several times a class period and clap his hands. The teacher did not believe that this was a tic, but rather a way for this boy to get other kids to laugh. When observed, this child was seen expending tremendous effort trying to hold his hand to the desk between each bout of clapping. This made it quite obvious that he didn't want to clap his hands and was not doing this simply to interrupt the class. Once it was understood that this was just a very complex motor tic, everyone quickly became used to it.

## Self-Abusive Tics

One young man had a tic that caused him to constantly hit himself very hard on both of his ears. It was clearly a tic, but more of what I call a "sensory tic." After months of repeating this tic, this young boy did irreparable damage to the hearing in both of his ears and is now wearing two hearing aids.

Another high school student had a sensory tic in which he would repeatedly slam his knuckle into his eye. Because this tic endured for many months, he ended up blinding himself in that eye. Both of these young men were helped by sensory therapy that was provided by an occupational therapist, which involved the use of weighted vests, blankets, and the like to provide the sensory input they were seeking to help calm down the tic.

A seventh grader named Cathy had several tics that caused considerable pain. One in particular was a wrist-twisting tic. The other involved hyperextending her arm. Because both these tics were causing bodily harm to muscles and tendons, she was forced at various times to wear wrist braces and also to keep her entire arm in an immobilizer sling so that she physically could not perform the tic. Of course, writing accommodations had to be made at school, because she was unable to write while wearing these devices.

One seven-year-old girl had a very hard coughing tic, which caused her a lot of chest pain. It got worse and worse until finally X-rays were taken. It was discovered that she had actually bruised ribs and caused one rib to grow too large for her chest cavity. She had to begin physical therapy to ease the terrible pain she was in. This same young girl also told me that timed math fact tests were her most difficult task at school. Usually students are given one minute to complete a certain number of math problems. This very wise girl said that if she could have just thirty extra seconds, she could finish. Her exact words were: "I figure that I spend about thirty seconds of that minute ticking, which the other kids don't have to do so with the extra thirty seconds, I would have the same time as everyone else." A seven-year old wise beyond her years, indeed!

## OCD and Anxiety

### The Clipboard Chronicle

John was a twelve-year-old student diagnosed with Tourette Syndrome (TS), obsessive-compulsive disorder (OCD), attention deficit hyperactivity disorder (ADHD), and several related learning disabilities. In seventh grade, he developed a socially very inappropriate tic-obsession. When he was in the presence of females, he would grab their breasts. Teachers first tried to modify the behavior with punishment. This was highly unsuccessful and actually made the tic worse by adding to John's stress. Interventions led to trying an environmental modification, which proved to be very effective. The child was first given permission to leave each class early, when there were no other students in the hallway. His seat was moved in every class so that he was surrounded by boys. That left the teachers to bear the brunt of the tic. Each teacher was asked to carry an especially large clipboard, which they could hold in front of themselves every time John approached them to have a conversation. (The bigger the clipboard, the better.) It actually became a sort of competition among the teachers to see who had the biggest, thickest clipboard. This humorous take on the situation served to change attitudes about John and his very difficult symptom. The clipboard took away the temptation, so to speak, and John did not do the tic if there was nothing to grab. All these steps also reduced John's anxiety about being punished for something that he truly could not control, and as the stress eased, so did the tic. We also did a peer in-service so that other students understood TS and were no longer fearful of John. These environmental modifications solved the problem.

## Dairy Dilemma

I myself once became obsessed with keeping the milk carton positioned perfectly straight on the refrigerator shelf. One morning I found myself back at the refrigerator for the eighth time to straighten the milk carton. I knew that if I didn't do something drastic, I would not get to school that morning. The only solution I could think of was to take the milk to work with me. The good news is that I bought donuts for my homeroom on the way to school and treated them to donuts and milk. They just thought I was a nice teacher and never realized that it was the only way to get out of my house that morning.

## Locker Phobia

A high school student became obsessed with checking the combination lock on his locker repeatedly to be sure that no one could break into his locker. As soon as that obsession started, he began arriving late for every class every day. He would make up excuses, saying that he didn't feel well and had gone to the bathroom or that he was fighting with his girlfriend. When the school social worker followed him from his homeroom one morning, she found that he had returned to check the combination lock on his locker forty-two times. The solution was quite simple: he bought a lock with a key.

## Toeing the Line

Anna was a seventh grader with TS, OCD, and some learning disabilities. She suddenly developed an obsession with her written work that required her to write every letter of every word perfectly on the lines of her paper. Night after night she was up until the wee hours of the morning copying and recopying her homework until every word was positioned exactly on the line. Her teachers struggled to find strategies and interventions. They thought of many things—providing a scribe, reducing the amount of homework, and so on. None seemed appropriate. Finally, we asked Anna what she thought would work. She came up with the best idea of all: why not simply allow her to use unlined paper? It worked! Going even further, we encouraged her to use a word processor, where everything looked perfect, and this further helped to solve the problem.

## Why Theresa Feels Trapped

Theresa, a middle school student, began to exhibit agitation for no apparent reason, which would frequently escalate into a confrontation with another student or sometimes even with the teacher. After many months, Theresa had developed a good relationship with a trusted counselor and confided that she often felt trapped in the classroom. She imagined that the door was locked and that she would not be able to get out of the room when it was time to go home. To relieve her anxiety, the classroom door was left open whenever possible. When this was not possible, she would sit close to the door with ongoing permission to get a drink of water whenever she felt the trapped feeling begin. After using this technique for a few days, she rarely left the room. Since she had permission to leave, she no longer felt trapped. This prevented her from becoming anxious, which reduced her difficult behaviors as well as her need to leave the room.

## Can You Hear Me Now?

A high school student suffered from debilitating tics that he tried very hard to suppress. He also suffered from OCD and anxiety. It became like a catch-22 situation. Trying to suppress symptoms caused great stress, which in turn caused the anxiety to worsen. The one thing that made the anxiety lessen was for him to be allowed to have his cell phone in his pocket. It was turned off and he didn't use it, but he needed to have it with him. The school had a policy that no student was allowed to carry a cell phone with him during the day. After many meetings, they finally agreed to allow him to carry the phone with him.

## What If I Choke?

My niece had many, many obsessive fears throughout her life. For a long period of time she could not sleep in her own bed. After this challenge went away, though, she became petrified of riding the school bus. When she was seventeen, she was babysitting at a neighbor's house and was eating potato chips when suddenly she started to choke on a potato chip. She drank some water and was fine. This single incident turned into an obsessive fear of eating anything. The situation worsened, and she was unable to eat anything at all for over three months, lost more than fifty pounds, and was in a life-threatening situation. It was only after she was properly diagnosed and prescribed a medication for OCD that she was able to start eating again.

## "But You Promised Chicken"

A mother related that as she put her ten-year-old on the school bus one morning, he asked her what was for dinner that night. She responded, "barbequed chicken." But as the mother was preparing to go to work, she forgot to take the chicken out of the freezer, so decided to make baked ham instead. When her son came home and saw that the meal had been changed, he went to his room and melted down for an hour throwing things around the room and crying uncontrollably. The mother asked me how she could possibly handle such a situation. My response was that she should never make that mistake again. She responded, "What mistake—making baked ham for dinner?" My response was no, the mistake she had made was telling him what was for dinner in the first place. Once he had barbequed chicken in his head, he couldn't shift gears, despite the fact that he loved baked ham.

This same boy's teacher related that he had made a rule that every day at 10:30 AM the class would have a snack time. If the teacher happened to be in the middle of correcting the last math problem at 10:30, this boy's hand would immediately be in the air. "Mr. J, it's 10:30. Mr. J, it's 10:31," and so on. Mr. J asked what he should do, and I said that he needed to change the rule. I suggested that every day when math was finished, the class would have snack time. That solved the problem. For children with OCD, the solution can be as simple as how you word something or how you respond to them.

## Kids Don't Tell

Although germ obsessions are the ones we hear about the most, OCD can take hundreds of other forms. A high school student became obsessed with counting things over and over again. With OCD, there is always doubt as to whether you did something right the first time, so you must do it repeatedly, just to be sure. This girl was actually compelled to count every word in every line that she read or wrote. She never shared with anyone what was going on and was soon failing all her classes. The more anxious she became, the worse the compulsion was. Everything she attempted to read or write took hours and hours. Once it was finally discovered what she was doing, we decided to provide her with a note taker and books on tape to enable her to finish her work.

When I was seven years old, I acquired a compulsion that caused me to read five words in my reader and then count to twenty-five in my head before I could go on to the next word. I was moved from the top reading group to several groups below because the teacher assumed that I simply did not know the next word. When I tell that story today, people inevitably ask me why I didn't simply tell the teacher what was going on in my head. There are two reasons why kids don't tell. First of all, you have nothing to compare it to. How did I know that other kids weren't doing the same thing in their head? Second, the biggest fear is that everyone will think you're crazy. You already feel crazy doing these ridiculous things over and over again.

## To the Point

A ten-year old boy developed an obsession with having a perfectly sharpened pencil at all times. He would interrupt the class sixteen or seventeen times every class period to resharpen his pencil. The solution was quite simple. We gave him twenty sharpened pencils at the beginning of every class. Two weeks later, the boy himself came up with an even better solution. He bought a mechanical pencil. Of course, the solution is not always this easy, but as an educator you should always be creative and keep an open mind.

## Thank God for Purell

As a French teacher, I traveled to Europe each summer with my students. On one of these trips, I had with me a thirteen-year-old boy who suffered from OCD. He had significant germ obsessions. One day he had to go to the bathroom very badly, but just could not go because there was no soap in the public bathroom. The only way I could persuade him to use the facilities was to give him some moist towelettes and a bottle of hand sanitizer that I had with me to disinfect his hands after he had used the bathroom.

## Scantron Saga

A high school student had several teachers who used the school's Scantron machine to grade their students' tests. This meant that students would take their test in the test booklet and then transfer the answers to the Scantron sheet. This girl was given extended time on tests, but couldn't finish them. When observed, she actually was finishing the test in the test booklet in plenty of time, but had an obsession with ensuring that every bubble on the Scantron sheet was filled in flawlessly. This process took hours. The simple solution was to allow her to take the test in the test booklet and have a teacher aide transfer her answers to the computer sheet. The teacher later agreed to correct the test booklet instead.

# Dysgraphia

## When Writing Hurts

Tom was a second grader with TS, ADHD, fine motor skills deficits, and OCD. He was very bright, but was struggling to keep up and was also becoming increasingly defiant and refusing to do his work. An observer noticed that Tom was always in motion—sometimes standing next to his desk or walking around it. Early on, his teacher had recognized Tom's need for movement and had placed his desk by the door, out of full view of the other students. When he moved about in his little space, no one else was disturbed and the movement helped him to pay attention (as is the case for most children with ADHD).

Despite the movement, Tom was very well behaved for the first two-thirds of the observation. Tom's problems began the minute the children were asked to "take out their papers and write a story." Tom played with things in his desk, went to his locker in the back of the room, to the bathroom, everything he could think of to avoid writing his story. Suddenly he went under his desk and refused to come out. The observer asked him why he was under there and what he was going to write about, and he immediately came up with his topic. When she asked him to come out from under his desk and write his opening sentence, the seven-year-old blurted out, "I can't write." The emotional power and overwhelming truth of the statement was not lost on the observer. She suggested to Tom that he dictate his story to her. She would be his "secretary" and write everything down for him. Immediately, his thoughts flowed freely. With a vocabulary well beyond that of a second grader, he completed six very good sentences in record time. He had the story in his head from the beginning, but like many students with TS, he simply could not get it onto paper.

Fine motor skill deficits and many interfering hand and finger tics made writing impossible and, indeed, for Tom, writing attempts had become very upsetting experiences. His handwriting was almost illegible, staying on the line was impossible, his margins were uneven, and every few words he had to stop, rest, and shake out his hand because it hurt so much. For Tom, the simplest solution was to refuse to write and avoid being upset and in pain. Today, he has an individualized education plan (IEP) with many writing supports, a scribe, his own laptop computer, and the amount of homework assigned to him has been reduced. His grades have improved dramatically, and he is a much happier child.

## Photo Op

I was working with a seventh grader who was having great difficulty getting his assignments copied down correctly. The team he was on had a policy of sending all the students back to their homeroom at the end of the day, where all the assignments for each of the classes were listed on the board. The students had five to seven minutes to copy down all the assignments. This young man could not copy the assignments down quickly enough or accurately. His grades were dropping because he was missing assignments or doing the wrong assignment. As we all sat and discussed possible solutions, this boy had the best suggestion of all. He asked permission to be able to take out his cell phone as soon as he arrived in the afternoon homeroom and take a picture of the assignments listed on the board. Problem solved!! He would then quickly download it to his computer, and the assignments were all copied and correct.

## To See or Not to See

I once taught a fifth grader with severe dysgraphia, which included visual motor difficulties. Since the French I taught in grade five was all oral, I had to become very creative when designing any type of evaluation. One of the first evaluations I gave was a test on colors in French. I had placed fifteen colored sheets of paper across the chalk tray with a number from one through fifteen above the sheets. The students had a piece of paper on their desks that was numbered from one through fifteen. I would say the color in French and the students would have to write the corresponding number from the board on their papers. After giving several examples of how this would work in English, we began the test.

This particular student, who seemed to know the colors very well in class each day when we practiced them, received a zero on the test. I called him up after class and decided to try to test him differently. I would say the color in French and he would have to bring me the piece of paper from the chalk tray that corresponded to the color I had said. Doing it this way, he scored 100 percent. I quickly realized that it was simply a visual motor problem and not a problem of him not knowing the material. From then on whenever we had a similar test, I would have him take it with the rest of the class and told him privately that it was just a practice test. We would then do the test together after class or during one of his free times. From that point on, he always got As in my class.

## Behavior Plans

### Hash Browns, French Fries, or Tater Tots: Any Kind of Potato Will Do

Pete was a sixth grader with TS, OCD, ADHD, and Asperger syndrome. As you can imagine, it was a challenge for his teachers to come up with creative solutions to meet his needs, but we were managing his tics, obsessions, and overactive behavior quite well. Our biggest challenge was how to manage the impulsive, inappropriate social behaviors he sometimes directed toward his peers and teachers. He was easily agitated and when in this emotional state, he would not only become verbally abusive but would act out physically as well—throwing any object that was close at hand out of frustration. We needed to find a positive way to help Pete get these behaviors under control. A behavior plan was set up targeting two behaviors: the verbal explosions and the throwing tantrums. First, we strategized with Pete about using more appropriate ways of expressing frustration. He was given a laminated pass to be able to leave the room whenever he felt he might commit either or both of the two bad behaviors. We practiced the strategy, but that worked only up to a point, the hurdle being finding a suitable reward. Nothing worked; everything we tried only interested him minimally, until one day we had a conversation with Pete and his special education teacher. For a half hour, he related his "profound" love of potatoes, expounding on every kind of potato he loved. Of course, this was the answer. As strange as it might seem, potatoes would be his reward.

With his mother's approval (and with her providing the potatoes), the last fifteen minutes of the day were potato time for Pete if his behavior chart had been good that day. We reviewed the chart with Pete frequently throughout the day so that he could regularly assess his progress toward his potatoes. If a day came when he had lost his potatoes by noon and we knew that the rest of the day had the potential of being a disaster, we started over and gave him the opportunity of earning at least half of them back. His behavior improved dramatically and he became lovingly known as "Potato Pete," a nickname he thoroughly enjoyed.

## The X Box Does It

An eighth-grade student with TS, OCD, and ADHD was having a difficult time debating what the teachers and other students were saying in class. It was that old "obsessive sense of justice" kicking in. The problem is that once he got started, he couldn't stop and the class would be disrupted for several minutes. We set up a behavior plan based on just that one behavior. It was called "No Debating." If he had an issue, he was allowed to bring it up to the teacher. The teacher would then quietly validate that he may have a point, but that she would prefer to discuss it with him privately after class. If he could then let it go, he would receive a plus for that class. For each five pluses he received, he would get a reward. We asked him what he wanted to work toward and he immediately said, "playing with my X Box at home." His mother agreed and for each five pluses, he would receive a fifteen-minute coupon to play his video game.

He was also given a special pass to be able to leave the room for three to four minutes as needed to help him put the issue to rest until after class. Because he was so vested in the reward, the plan worked very well, and many times by the end of class he had forgotten all about what he wanted to debate.

## Miscellaneous

### I Like Ben Better

Ben was an eighth grader with TS, ADHD, OCD, and learning disabilities. When his class schedule arrived in the mail before school started in September, he observed that he had five academic classes in a row before lunch, with no break. And because he was an eighth grader, he had the last lunch period at 1:10 PM. By the time he arrived at his last class, it was nearly impossible for him to sit still and pay attention and his tics were at an all-time high. The teacher of that class quickly realized this and decided to have a private meeting with Ben to brainstorm about possible solutions. It was her suggestion that Ben would report to her class, put his materials on his desk, and leave to take a five-minute walk to the drinking fountain, bathroom, and so forth, to release tics and get a bit of exercise. This break hopefully would assist him in attending better and ticking less when he returned to class. The first five minutes of class were usually spent taking attendance, passing back papers, and such, so with this plan he would not miss any of the lesson.

However, in about a week's time, the inevitable happened. Ben arrived five minutes after class had begun, as usual. One student raised her hand and asked why Ben was always allowed to come to class late. The teacher had not prepared for such questions, so simply answered, "Because I like Ben better." The other students were speechless. They knew in their hearts that this was not true, but did not know how to respond. They also knew about Ben's TS. Nothing more was said until later in the class, when the teacher directed the students back to her off-the-cuff comment. She used it as "teachable moment" and communicated to them a very important lesson: *what's fair is not always equal, and what's equal is not always fair.* Each student gets what he needs, and it may never be the same as other students' treatment. She compared it to a child with diabetes who needed to have a snack in the middle of the morning. Did that mean that everyone had a snack? Certainly not. No one ever asked again why Ben came in late or why anyone else in the class seemed to be favored at any given time. It was a lesson well learned.

# Executive Dysfunction

## A Shoe Will Do

When I entered my twentieth year of teaching several years ago, I made the conscious decision not to "sweat the small stuff." I gave up worrying about kids who forgot their pencils, rulers, and such. I would simply lend them one. I find that the majority of kids who continually forget or lose their supplies are kids with ADHD and executive dysfunction. They are not forgetting things on purpose; they simply have a neurological disorder that prevents them from remembering. So why lose sleep over such a petty thing? We don't punish hearing-impaired kids because they can't hear or visually impaired kids because they can't see, so why would we punish these kids because they forget their pencils? Take a shoe as ransom for what you lent them to make sure that you get the pencil back. (A word of warning, though—I have seen kids with these disorders leave the room without their shoe.) Teach them strategies. Life is too short to worry about pencils.

## Circling the Wagons

I once assigned a project to my eighth graders that involved making a large movie poster in French (I was a French teacher) about their favorite movie. The poster was to contain the name of the movie, the theater and times where it would be showing, the type of movie it was, and several *Siskel and Ebert*–type critiques about the film. I divided the class into groups of two and spent ten minutes going over the detailed and color-coded project sheet that I had given them. I then set out on various tables in the classroom piles of poster board, magic markers, and other supplies that they would need for the project. They were then ready to start work, which 99 percent of the class did immediately. The one exception was Sam. Sam had TS, OCD, ADHD, and executive dysfunction, and he did what all children with these disorders do when given a large long-term project to do: he began circling the room. He was at the marker table, then the poster board table, pulling the ears of other students, and generally wreaking havoc in the room.

I approached him and asked him what he was looking for, to which he responded, "poster board." I then asked him what he was going to write on the poster board. He had no response, but instead changed his story, saying that he was looking for markers to use. I asked him again what he would be writing with the markers. Again, no response. As simple as it sounds to most of us, this boy could not even begin to tell me what step one of the project should be until I reminded him that he was supposed to be doing a poster on his favorite movie. He had neglected to start by selecting a movie.

I worked side by side with Sam throughout that class period and the next. With my guidance, he found pictures on the computer, typed up his comments, and made good progress. Each day as he left class, I took what he had accomplished and put it in a special folder on my desk. (I knew that if I let him take it with him, I would never see it again.) When we were no longer working on the project in class, I had him come to my room during his lunchtime so he could finish it. Normally this would be the responsibility of the resource room teacher, but since she did not know any French, it fell on me. Sam's final poster was fantastic! The French was perfect, and he received an A. A week later was the school's annual parents' night. All the posters were displayed on my classroom wall, including Sam's. I looked toward the back of the room at one point in the evening, and there was Sam's mother standing by his poster with tears in her eyes. When I approached her and asked if she was OK, she answered that this was the first time that Sam had ever had a project displayed in any classroom. He never finished one. She then said to me, "Sam didn't really do this, did he?" to which I responded, "He certainly did, and I have many new grey hairs to prove it."

Sam was a very bright, creative child who just happened to have executive dysfunction. With the correct guidance, he could accomplish just about anything.

I want to extend an enthusiastic thank-you to all the wonderful educators, counselors, and administrators I have met over my many years working with children with these disorders. I can attest to the fact that there are some very caring, very creative, and very hardworking people working in our schools across the country. You know who you are and may have taught one of the children written about in this section. I know how difficult your job can be under ideal circumstances. Thank you for inviting me into your classroom and allowing me to work with you to help a child with these disorders. I am a grown-up child who did not always have such caring teachers.

# Index

## A

Acceptance, setting an example of, 139
Accommodation plan, *See* 504
    Accommodation Plan
Activities schedule, 123
ADA, *See* Americans with Disabilities Act
    (ADA),
ADHD, *See* Attention deficit hyperactivity
    disorder (ADHD)
Americans with Disabilities Act (ADA),
    127, 132–133
Antihypertensive medications, 18
Anxiety: disorders, 21; and OCD,
    118–119, 153–158; and tics, 12, 101
Aripiprazole (Abilify©), 18
Asperger syndrome, 21
Assignments, *See also* Homework: and
    executive dysfunction, 122–123;
    providing alternatives for, 120; quality
    vs. quantity, 120; structuring, 123
Assistive technology evaluation,
    requesting, 121
Associated disorders, 21–47;
    accommodations for, 116–125;
    anxiety disorders, 21; attention deficit
    hyperactivity disorder (ADHD), 21–23;
    auditory processing deficits, 34,
    121–122; behavior issues, 21, 36–38;
    depression, 21, 29; dysgraphia, 21,
    24–26; and executive dysfunction,
    21, 27–28, 122–124; fine-motor
    difficulties, 21, 24–26; learning
    disabilities, 33; obsessive-compulsive
    disorder (OCD), 21, 39–47; repeated
    anger-generated episodes (RAGE), 21;
    sensory processing, 21, 31–32; sleep
    disorders, 21, 30, 69, 71; social skills
    deficits, 21, 35; social skills training,
    125; social stories, 125
Attention Deficit Disorder Association
    web site, 143
Attention deficit hyperactivity disorder
    (ADHD), 21–23; disorganization,
    23; hyperactivity, 22; impulsiveness,
    22; inattentiveness, 22; socially
    immaturity, 23
Auditory processing deficits, 34, 121–122
Autism spectrum, overlaps with TS, 21

## B

Background noises, 34, 121
Behavior issues, 21, 36–38; accommoda-
    tions for, 117; precipitating factors,
    37–38
Behavior plans, real-life scenarios,
    161–163
Binders, 83
Biofeedback, 140
Blackboard (software), 74, 120
Brain chemical imbalance, and vocal
    tics, 11
Bupropion (Welbutrin©), and OCD, 46

## C

Children and Adults with Attention
    Deficit/Hyperactivity Disorder web
    site, 143
Chronic motor or vocal tic disorder,
    16–17
Citalopram (Celexa©), and OCD, 46
Class notes, providing, 120
Classmates, educating about TS,
    93–97

Classroom: Classroom Observation Form, 104; dealing with tics in, 98; environment, 100
Clonidine (Catapres), 18
Clothing, and sensory issues, 70-71
Cognitive behavioral therapy (CBT), 47
Color coding, 123
Communication: with parents, 100; between school and parents, 79, 88
Complex motor tics, 8
Complex vocal tics, 9-11
Comprehensive Behavioral Intervention for Tics (CBIT), 19
Compulsions, 39-40, 56, 119
Coping mechanism, sense of humor as, 2
Coprolalia, 10, 101
Coughing tic, 152-153
Council for Exceptional Children web site, 143
Creativity, and OCD, 119
Cursing, 150-151

**D**

Depression, 21, 29
Diagnostic criteria, TS, 6
Disabilities Education Act (IDEA), 137-138
Disney's Adventures in Typing with Timon and Pumba, 77
Distraction: and obsession, 70, 118; and OCD, 118
Dopamine, 5-6
Dragon Speak Naturally (Nuance), 121
Dysgraphia, 21, 24-26, 33, 73, 88, 119, 131; characteristics of, 24; classroom difficulties for children with, 25-26; diagnosis of, 24; and handwriting, 25-26; real-life scenarios, 159-161

**E**

Echolalia, 10
Educational rights of students, with TS/OCD, 127
Eisenreich, J., 97
Environment, 88-89; accommodations, 100; and sensory issues, 70-71

Escitalopram (Lexapro©), and OCD, 46
Excitement, and tics, 12, 101
Executive dysfunction, 21, 27-28; and assignments, 122-123; and associated disorders, 122-124; defined, 27; real-life scenarios, 164-166
Exercise, 71
Eye blinking, 13, 14, 96

**F**

Fatigue, and tics, 13, 101
Fine-motor difficulties, 21; See also Dysgraphia
Finger tics, 100
504 Accommodation Plan, 74, 79, 127, 132-133
Fluoxetine (Prozac©), and OCD, 46
Fluvoxamine (Luvox©), and OCD, 46
Functional Behavioral Assessment (FBA), 105-108
Functional behavioral assessment worksheet: for student with TS and associated disorders, 109-111; summary of, 111-112

**G**

Garcia, M., 125
Germ obsession, 43, 56-57, 117, 158
Ginnott, Haim, 139
Gray, C., 125
Green, R. W., 141
Guanfacine (Tenex), 18

**H**

Haloperidol (Haldol), 18
Hand tic, 100; real-life scenario, 148
Handwriting, 24, 25-26, 120
Head jerking tics, 96
Headset, use of, 71, 73, 117, 122
Help/support sources, 142
Holding in tics, 14-15
Home Behavior Assessment worksheet, 65-68
Homework, 88, 120-121; assignments, providing alternatives for, 120;

breaking down assignments into manageable parts, 73, 122; buddy, 74, 123; and computers, 73; managing, 73–75, 88–89; school's web site, 74; wind-down time before, 71
Howard, T., 97
Humor, and OCD, 118
Hyposensitivity, sensory, 31

## I

IDEA, *See* Individuals with Disabilities Act (IDEA)
IEP, *See* Individualized education plan (IEP)
Illness, and tics, 12
Index cards, use of, 121; and homework, 73
Individualized education plan (IEP), 74, 79; sample letter for requesting, 84; synopsis of, 79–81
Individuals with Disabilities Act (IDEA), 128–131; defined, 128; need for services, 128; qualifying for IEP under, 128; reauthorization of, 129–130; refusal for classification, 129; Section 300.324, 129; and TS, 129–131
Inspirations (software), 121
Involuntary movements/vocalizations, 5–6

## J

Johnson, S., 97
Joshua Center for Neurological Disorders (Kansas City, Mo.) web site, 143
JumpStart Typing, 77

## L

Learning disabilities, 21, 33
Learning Disabilities Association of America web site, 143
Letters requesting services, 83–84, 135–136

## M

Mandell, H., 97
Mavis Beacon Learn to Type, 77

Medical treatment of TS, 18–20; clonidine (Catapres), 18; Comprehensive Behavioral Intervention for Tics (CBIT), 19; guanfacine (Tenex), 18; haloperidol, 18; medication side effects, 19
Meditation, 140
Meltdowns, 65
Motor tics, 7–8, 141; accommodating, 99–100; chronic, 16–17; clapping tic, 151–152; complex, 8; leg jerking tic, 149; real-life scenarios, 148–153; simple, 7; touching body parts in order, 151; twirling tic, 151

## N

National Center for Learning Disabilities web site, 143
National Information Clearinghouse for Handicapped Children and Youth (NICHCY) web site, 143
Neuroleptic medication, 18
Neurological disorders, complexity of, 105
New Jersey Center for Tourette Syndrome web site, 143

## O

Obsession, 39, 73, 88; and distraction, 70
Obsessive-compulsive disorder (OCD), xix, 21; accentuating the positive, tips for, 59; acting as role model for children with, 137–138; and anxiety, 153–158; behavioral interventions for, 47; behavioral issues, accommodating, 117–118; careful wording for children with, 157; cell phone obsession, 155; checking things over and over, 41–42, 55–56; choking fear, 156; clipboard chronicle, 153; constant doubt/worrying, 56; counting obsession, 157; counting obsessions, 41, 55; dairy dilemma, 154; discipline for symptoms of, 1; educating peers about, 91–92; ensuring success at school, tips for, 60–61; family, impact on, 50–52; germ obsession, 158; germs/contamination,

43, 56–57; hidden nature of, 1; locker phobia, 154; manifestations of, 10 15; medical treatment of, 16; misdiagnosis of, 1; obsessive fears, 42–43, 56; obsessive sense of justice, 45, 58, 117; obsessive thoughts, 45, 58; peer in-service model, 93–97; pencil-sharpening obsession, 158; recognition of, 49; repeated questions, asking, 43–44, 57; ritualistic behaviors, 43, 57; Scantron machine scenario, 158; school performance, impact on, 55–58; symmetry/perfectionism/neatness, 40–41, 55; toeing the line, 154–155; training all staff, 90; transitions/change, difficulty, 44–45, 57; trapped feelings, 155; word-counting obsession, 157

Obsessive Compulsive Foundation, 143

Occupational therapy (OT) intervention, 119

OCD Foundation, 142

Olanzapine (Zyprexia©), 18

Organization web sites, 143–144

**P**

Pallilalia, 10

Parent Advocacy Center for Educational Rights web site, 144

Parent checklists, 62–84; Accommodations, Tips, and Environmental Changes, 69–72; Home Behavior Assessment worksheet, 65–68; homework, managing, 73–75, 88–89; positive behavioral management and supports, 65–68; school breaks/rainy weekends/summer vacation, 76–78; school issues, 79; supporting children with TS and OCD, 63–64

Parent Training and Information Center (PTI), 82; web site, 144

Parkinson's disease: symptoms of, 5–6; and TS, 5

Paroxetine (Paxil©), and OCD, 46

Peers: educating about TS/OCD, 91–92; in-service model, 93–97

Pennsylvania Tourette Syndrome Alliance web site, 143

Pervasive developmental disorder, 21

Photocopying materials, 121

Physician's letter (sample), 135–136

Physicians referral lists, 19

Pimozide (Orap©), 18

Playground, aide's role in, 116

Positive Behavior Intervention Plan (PBIP), 105–108; for student with TS, 113–115

Praise, offering for homework accomplishment, 73

**R**

RAGE, *See* Repeated anger-generated episodes (RAGE)

Read, Write & Type, 77

Real-life scenarios, 147–166; behavior plans, 161–163; dysgraphia, 159–161; executive dysfunction, 164–166; hand tic, 148; miscellaneous, 163–164; motor tics, 148–153; Scantron machine real-life scenario, 158; tapping tic, 148; vocal tics, 148–153

Red flags, identifying, 119

Relaxation techniques, 140

Repeated anger-generated episodes (RAGE), 21, 65

Reports, providing alternatives for, 120

Requesting services, 134; sample physician's letter, 135–136

Risperidone (Risperdal©), 18

**S**

Sample physician's letter, 135–136

Scantron machine real-life scenario, 158

School(s): assemblies, child's seat during, 116; and blame, 61; breaks/summer vacation, 76–78; cooperation, 60–61; daily communication system, 60; ensuring success at, 60–61; evaluation, if parents disagree with, 137; issues, 79; and OCD, 118; placement, 141

Scribe, 120

Self-abuse tics, 152–153

Sense of humor, as coping mechanism, 2
Sensory defensiveness, 21
Sensory hypersensitivity, 31–32
Sensory hyposensitivity, 31
Sensory issues, 34, 70–71; accommodations for, 116–117
Sensory processing, 31–32
Sensory tics, 152–153
Sertraline (Zoloft©), and OCD, 46
Simple motor tics, 7
Simple vocal tics, 9
Skype, 102
Slam Dunk Typing, 77
Sleep disorders, 21, 30, 69, 71
Social skills: deficits, 21, 35; training, 125
Social stories, 125
Spelling/spelling errors, 24, 26, 120
Spitting tic, 100
SSRIs (selective serotonin reuptake inhibitors), and OCD, 46
Stress, 101; and OCD, 118; supports to reduce, 118; and tics, 12, 101
Student attitude, toward vocal tics, 103
Study guides, 74
Super Mario Learns to Type, 77
Suppression of symptoms, TS, 14–15

**T**

Tapping tic, real-life scenario, 148
Teacher attitude, toward vocal tics, 103
Teacher checklists, 85–125; Classroom Observation Form, 104; dealing with tics in the classroom, 98; educating peers, 91–92; major components of TS, 85–86; motor tics, accommodating, 99–100; peer in-service model, 93–97; training all staff, 90; vocal tics, 101–103
*Teacher Looks at Tourette Syndrome, A* (DVD), 90
Teachers: composure, 118; top ten things to know about TS, 86–87
Tests, providing alternatives for, 120
Thumb drive, 124
Tics, 33, 73, 88, 96–97, 99, 140–141, *See* Motor tics; Vocal tics; Comprehensive Behavioral Intervention for Tics

(CBIT), 19; dealing with in the classroom, 98; and sleep, 71
TICS of Georgia web site, 143
Tolerance, setting an example of, 139
Tourette Syndrome Association (TSA), 19–20, 81, 83, 90, 142; associated disorders, 21–47; autism spectrum, overlaps with TS, 21; defined, 85; major components of TS, 85–86; web site, 143
Tourette Syndrome (TS): acting as role model for children with, 137–138; alignment with bad behavior, 1; characteristics of, 5; childhood onset of, 13; defined, 5; diagnosis of, 6; as disability of disinhibition, 11; discipline for symptoms of, 1; educational rights of students, 127; family, impact on, 50–52; frequency, by gender, 5; genetic basis of, 5; medical treatment of, 18–20, 88; misdiagnosis of, 1; recognition of, 49; school performance, impact on, 53–54; suppression of symptoms, 14–15; symptoms of, xix, 5; top ten things teachers need to know about, 86–87; understanding, 15; waxing and waning of symptoms, 12–13, 60
Training staff, 90
Transient tic disorder, 16
Transitions/transition warnings, 69, 117–118
Trapper Keeper binders, 77, 82

**V**

Venlafaxine (Effexor©), and OCD, 46
Visuals, use of, 72, 121
Vocal tics, 141; accommodating, 102–103; and brain chemical imbalance, 11; chronic, 16–17; complex, 9–11; coprolalia, 10, 101; cursing, 150–151; dealing with, 101; echolalia, 10; "I have a chicken in my pants" tic, 148–149; manifestations of, 9–11; pallilalia, 10; "peanut butter" tic, 149; real-life scenarios, 148–153; simple, 9; teacher/student attitudes toward, 103
Voice-activated computer software, 121

## W

Waxing and waning of symptoms, TS, 12–13, 60
Wind-down time, before homework, 71
Word bank, 123
Wrist-twisting tic, 152

## Y

Yoga, 140

## Z

Ziprasidone (Geodon©), 18